W9-AHJ-508

HyperStudio Design:	Roger Wagner and Michael O'Keefe
HyperStudio Programmers:	Michael O'Keefe, Chris Arsenault and Loren Wright
Contributing Programmers:	Mike Westerfield, Ken Kashmarek, and Rick Chapman
Graphic Artists:	Jeff Kelley and Donald McIntosh
HyperStudio Reference:	Tony Latess
HyperStudio Tutorial:	Maureen Gross
Dedicated To:	Pam Wagner and Andrea Marcucci

Roger Wagner Publishing, Inc.

1050 Pioneer Way, Suite P

El Cajon, California 92020

© Copyright 1988-1995 by Roger Wagner Publishing, Inc.

Document Code: AMMB 7-95

ISBN 0-927796-49-X
1995 96 97 98   8 7 6 5 4 3 2

Customer Licensing Agreement

The Roger Wagner Publishing, Inc. software product that you have just received from Roger Wagner Publishing, Inc., or one of its authorized dealers, is provided to you subject to the "Terms and Conditions of the Software Customer Licensing Agreement. Should you decide that you cannot accept these Terms and Conditions, then you must return your product with all documentation and this License marked "REFUSED" within the 30 day examination period following the receipt of the product.

1. License. Roger Wagner Publishing, Inc.. hereby grants you upon your receipt of this product, a non-exclusive license to use the enclosed Roger Wagner Publishing, Inc. product subject to the terms and restrictions set forth in this License Agreement.

2. Copyright. This software product, and its documentation, is copyrighted by Roger Wagner Publishing, Inc., with all rights reserved. You may not copy or otherwise reproduce the product or any part of it except as expressly permitted in this License.

3. Restrictions on Use and Transfer. The original and any backup copies of this product are intended for your own personal use (one person) in connection with no more than two computers (for example, one at home and one at work). You may not sell or transfer copies of, or any part of, this product, nor rent or lease to others without the express written permission of Roger Wagner Publishing, Inc.

Limitations of Warranties and Liability

Roger Wagner Publishing, Inc. and the program author shall have no liability or responsibility to purchaser or any other person or entity with respect to liability, loss or damage caused or alleged to be caused directly or indirectly by this software, including, but not limited to any interruption of service, loss of business or anticipatory profits or consequential damages resulting from the use or operation of this software. Some states do not allow the exclusion or limitation of implied warranties or liability for incidental or consequential damages, so the above limitation or exclusion may not apply to you.

Sharing HyperStudio Stacks With Others

HyperStudio stacks are normally used with the full HyperStudio software, but there are times when you may wish to share your stacks with others who do not already own the HyperStudio software.

Although you are not permitted to give copies of the full HyperStudio software to others, you can share your stacks with others using the **"HyperStudio Player"** application, which is included in this package. Please see your HyperStudio manual for more information on this option.

The License below grants you, as a legitimate purchaser of the HyperStudio package, the right to make and distribute copies of **"The HyperStudio Player"**, provided that each copy is for non-profit purpose, and that each copy of **"The HyperStudio Player"** is accompanied by a copy of one or more stacks that you have created with HyperStudio. The purpose of the copy must be to permit another user to view your stacks. A license to copy and distribute **"The HyperStudio Player"** along with your stacks for commercial purposes is available from Roger Wagner Publishing, Inc. Please contact Roger Wagner Publishing, Inc. if you require a copy of the Commercial Use Licensing Agreement.

The HyperStudio Player License Agreement

The purchaser of this HyperStudio package (the Licensee) has the right to make, authorize to make, and distribute copies of the presentation-oriented program entitled **"The HyperStudio Player"**, which is included as part of the HyperStudio package; provided, however, that each copy:

(1) is made for purposes of accompanying a copy of a stack or group of stacks created by the Licensee;
(2) is made only for the purpose of permitting others to view the stack or group of stacks created by the Licensee;
(3) is made only for non-profit purposes, and
(4) includes all notices found in the original, including but not limited to the Roger Wagner Publishing, Inc. copyright notice.

A commercial-purpose license is available from Roger Wagner Publishing, Inc. and must be obtained before you can distribute the HyperStudio Player for commercial purposes.

Table of Contents

Reference

Chapter Three – Cards   17

Chapter Four – Buttons   25

Chapter Seven – Sound 73

Chapter Eight – Animation   79

Chapter Nine – QuickTime   85

Chapter Ten – Windows   89

Appendix C – VCR As A Printer   141

Appendix D – Memory & Disk Use   145

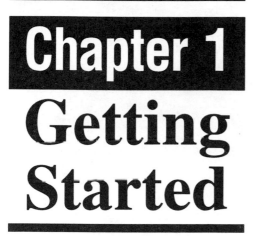

Chapter 1
Getting Started

The HyperStudio Package

Inside the HyperStudio box, you should find the following:

- HyperStudio application installation disks.
- HyperStudio System CD-ROM.
- HyperStudio Tutorial & Reference (this book).
- HyperLogo Tutorial & Reference.
- HyperStudio Registration Card (Very important!)
- Additional printed support materials.

The HyperStudio System CD-ROM contains a collection of over 200mb of clip-art and clip-sounds that you may use in your own stacks and over 100mb of sample stacks to show you what others are doing with HyperStudio. Although the CD is not required at any given moment during the use of HyperStudio, its resources will prove invaluable to any stack project that you are working on, so you should keep it close at hand.

System Requirements

HyperStudio requires a Macintosh running on either System 6 or later. It will run on stand-alone machines, and, if you have the "multi-user" version, networks as well! If you've got a "happy Mac" when you start up your computer, you can run HyperStudio! A CD-ROM drive is highly recommended (for installation, and access to the extensive resource library), but not absolutely required.

To install HyperStudio, you should also have 15mb of free disk space on your hard disk, and 2mb of free RAM at the Finder when your computer has started up.

If you do not have the disk or memory space as suggested above, or do not have a CD-ROM drive, you can probably still use HyperStudio! Please read Appendix X,

"HyperStudio Disk & Memory Use", for more information, and suggestions on how to adjust the installation of HyperStudio to best suit your system.

Installing the Software

Installing the software is simple, and consists of these basic steps:

1. Drag the folder HyperStudio for HD from the CD-ROM disk to your hard disk.

2. Use the HyperStudio Installation diskettes to put the actual HyperStudio application into the HyperStudio for HD folder.

For the exact installation instructions, please locate and read the "Installing HyperStudio" booklet that was also included with this package.

Technical Support

If you have any questions during the installation process, or have questions that this documentation does not cover, please let us be of help!. You can call our technical support hotline, at:

(619) 442-0522 Extension 13

9:30am - 5:30pm Pacific

Monday through Friday

Please have your serial number ready.

We'll be happy to help you!

Chapter 2
Stacks

What Are Stacks?

A *stack* is a file that contains one or more cards, along with any buttons, graphics, sounds, and other multimedia elements that have been placed on those cards. The chapters that follow this one will tell you more about each of those elements, but if you've even looked at the Home Stack by now, then you probably already have the general idea.

Keep in mind that an entire project may be made up of several stacks, linked together through buttons. In general, a stack has all the information contained within the particular file, such as graphics, sounds and text. The main exception to this are QuickTime movies, which are not stored within your stack file, due to their size. Instead, "pointers" are kept within your stack to any movies used by that stack.

This is important to remember when you want to move one or more stacks to another disk: QuickTime movies called by that stack must be moved along with the files as well.

Unless you specifically tell HyperStudio to keep other data elements separate from your stack, everything other than QuickTime movies will be contained in your stack, and moving the individual file moves all the elements associated with it. (See the chapters on sound, text and graphics to learn about how to deliberately make the data files separate).

Working With Stacks

Opening An Existing Stack

When you start up HyperStudio, the first thing it will do is try to find a stack to open. In this case, it is one named "Home Stack". If you have put the HyperStudio application in a folder that doesn't have a Home Stack, you will be presented with a dialog box (called the Standard File Selection dialog in this manual), which asks you to locate a stack for HyperStudio to begin with.

However, in normal practice, starting HyperStudio delivers you to the Home Stack. From there you have two ways of opening a stack.

The first, and most usual way, is to just choose "Open Stack" from the File menu. This will give you the Standard File Selection dialog, from which you can open any stack file on any disk or CD. Only stack files are shown in this dialog, so you don't have to worry about opening any file that is not a stack.

The second way of opening a stack is to create a button in a given stack that connects to any other stack you wish. See the chapter on Buttons for specific information on how to do this.

NOTE: In the case of the Home Stack supplied with HyperStudio, a special button is provided right on the main Home Stack screen, which will bring up the Standard File Selection dialog to open a stack. (This button was created using the New Button Action ("NBA") MenuChooser. See the discussion later in this chapter for more information about how that was done.)

Starting a New Stack

Starting a new stack is easy: just choose "New Stack" from the File menu!

When you start a new stack, you'll see the first card of your stack, which will have a white background. If you have not checked "Experienced User" in the HyperStudio Preferences section, you'll also get a dialog box telling you just what's happened. This help note only appears the first time you create a new stack in any particular session with HyperStudio.

As a special Home Stack feature, there is also an automated "Start a New Stack" button on the main Home Stack Card. Like the "Open Stack" button, this just uses the MenuChooser NBA to do what you would have done manually: choose New Stack from the File menu.

Saving a Stack for the First Time: Save As

You should save your stack files not only when you're done working on them, but also as you work. By saving often, you keep the option open of re-opening a version of your stack which was saved before you made the last group of changes. You also protect the work you've done in the event of an unexpected problem with your computer.

When a stack is saved for the very first time, you need to give the stack a name, and tell HyperStudio where you would like the stack to be stored on your hard disk. This is done with Save Stack As from the File menu.

When you choose "Save Stack As…," from the File menu, the standard file dialog is shown.

Compared to "Open Stack…", you'll see a new item: a text entry line at the bottom of the dialog where you name your stack. (If your stack hasn't been named yet, the default name shown will be "Untitled".) Above this box, all of the files in the current folder are shown, in dimmed text. This is so you can see which names are already used.

After giving it a name, simply press Return or click the "Save" button to complete the operation.

If you create a new stack, and choose Save, rather than "Save As", before you've given your stack a name, HyperStudio will automatically act as though you'd chosen "Save As", and give you the file dialog for naming your stack, and choosing a location for it.

File	
New Stack	
Open Stack...	⌘O
Save Stack	⌘S
Save Stack As...	
Import Background...	⌘I
Export Screen...	⌘E
Add Clip Art...	⌘A
Page Setup...	
Print...	⌘P
Print to Video...	
Quit HyperStudio	⌘Q

▲▲▲

When saving your stack for the first time you can use the Save Stack As… option.

Saving a Stack While You Work: Save Stack

Once the stack file has been saved for the first time (and thus has a name and location), you can save your work with just the "Save Stack" command. HyperStudio remembers the stack's name and location, so you don't need to use "Save As" again, unless you want to create a second copy of the stack file in a new location and/or with a new name.

A good habit to develop is pressing Command-S (the keyboard shortcut for "Save Stack") any time that you pause in your stack development, or any time you make a large change to your stack, for example, after drawing a complex background or editing a large Text Object.

Moving or Deleting Stacks

Eventually, you may want to move your stack files to another location, or even delete files that you no longer want. Both these operations are best done with the "Finder". The Finder is the desktop environment of the Macintosh, where you can manipulate folders and files using the mouse. If you are unsure how to use the Finder to manipulate files, see your Macintosh manual for more information.

In general, if you have a group of stacks in a folder, they can be moved to any new location you wish by just dragging the entire folder, or by moving whichever stacks you are interested in to an existing folder.

Remember that QuickTime movies are kept as separate files, and must be moved with your stack if the stack is being moved to a different computer, or any situation where the original QuickTime movie file will not be "online" when your stack is used. In those cases, simply place the QuickTime movie file in the same folder as the stack that will be using it.

The Home Stack

The Home Stack is a special case of a HyperStudio stack, in two ways:

1. HyperStudio looks for a stack named "Home Stack" in the same directory as the application when it first starts up.

2. Whenever HyperStudio opens a stack with the name "Home Stack", it specifically remembers where it is, so that a later Home Stack button action, or choosing "Home" from the "Move" menu will instantly return you to the exact position within that Home Stack that you last visited.

The default Home Stack is installed on your hard drive during the normal HyperStudio installation procedure. It tells you a little bit about multimedia and HyperStudio helps you locate other stacks on your disk. The Home Stack is usually a "menu" style stack that has connections to all the other stacks in your system.

Making Your Own Home Stack

You may want to eventually replace the provided Home Stack with one of your own making that better suits your needs. To do this, simply name your stack Home Stack and place it in the same folder as HyperStudio. It will automatically be loaded on startup and by pressing Command-H, the user will be returned to your Home Stack.

If you receive a stack set from a friend that includes a stack called Home Stack, you want to be careful to not replace your usual Home Stack with the new file. In most cases, you will want to create a new folder when you receive a group of stacks that all work together and have their own Home Stack.

For example, let's say you've received a disk containing a French Poodle Information stack. Examining the folder shows four HyperStudio stacks: Home Stack, Grooming, Feeding, and Attitude. You know that these four stacks work together and through experimentation (or by a lucky guess), you decide that starting the French Poodle Information stack is as simple as opening the file Home Stack.

One of the easiest ways to install this on a hard drive is to make a folder in your HyperStudio folder called Poodle Stacks, and copy all of the files from the hard drive into the new folder. You could then make a button on your Home Stack that connects to the stack called Home Stack inside of the Poodle Stacks folder.

To return from the French Poodle Information stack to your original Home Stack (which resides in the same folder as the HyperStudio application), you need to make a button in the French Poodle home stack that connects back to your own Home Stack. You can't simply make a button with a button action of "Connect to home stack" because the most recently loaded stack named Home Stack was the French Poodle Information Home Stack—and as a result, the button marked "Connect to Home Stack" won't go anyplace.

There are two ways to avoid all of this. The first is to design your multi-stack sets so that the "main" stack (which accesses the others) is called "Poodles Start", or something similarly obvious to users, but not named "Home Stack". So, for the example above, ideally, the stack that began the French Poodle Information set should have been called Poodles Start. This would have avoided having to place a special button in the Poodle Home file to return to your original home stack—a simple "Connect to home stack" would have gone to the main HyperStudio Home Stack (since it was the last stack loaded that was named Home Stack).

The second solution is to put a button in the French Poodle Information Home Stack and use "Connect to another stack…", to link it to your regular (main) HyperStudio Home Stack.

```
╔══════════ About stack - Home Stack ══════════╗
║  ┌─────────────────────────┐  ┌─ Things to do when: ──┐ ║
║  │ Number of cards:     1  │  │ ☐ arriving at this stack... │ ║
║  │ Current memory used: 2 K│  │ ☐ leaving this stack...     │ ║
║  │ Disk space needed:   2 K│  │ ☐ clicking on this stack... │ ║
║  │ Available memory:  2008 K│ └───────────────────────┘ ║
║  └─────────────────────────┘                          ║
║  ┌─────────────────────────┐   Cursor:  [ ⊕ ▼ ]       ║
║  │ Number of colors:  256  │                          ║
║  │ Card width:        512  │                          ║
║  │ Card height:       342  │   ┌────────┐ ┌──────────┐║
║  │ [Change # of colors or size...] │ Cancel │ │    OK    │║
║  └─────────────────────────┘   └────────┘ └──────────┘║
╚═══════════════════════════════════════════════╝
```

▲▲▲

The Stack Information dialog.

Stack Information

To get information on the stack you are in, choose "About this Stack" under the Objects menu. This command provides information about the entire stack. It includes the size of the stack in memory, and how many cards are in the stack. It also reports the amount of memory that the stack currently occupies in the machine, how much space it requires on disk, and how much memory is available in the machine. The number of colors the stack is set to use is also reported here along with the card width and card height.

Changing the Number of Colors

You can change the number of colors you'd like to work with in your stack, by choosing "About this Stack " from the Objects menu. "Click on the Change # of colors or size" button to choose a b&w, 16 or 256-color stack.

Sharing Stacks

Although the HyperStudio program itself cannot be given to others, you can give out copies of a miniature version of HyperStudio (sometimes called the "run-time version") that has no editing functions. This program is called HyperStudio Player and can be found in a folder called "My Stacks" along with a mini Home Stack ready to be customized for your own use.

Simply place your stack (named Home Stack) on a data disk along with the HyperStudio Player (the run-time version of HyperStudio). The user can launch the HyperStudio Player from the Finder.

Note that if the eventual user of your stack will own HyperStudio, there is no need for the HyperStudio Player—they can simply load your stack with their copy of HyperStudio.

Although there is no license fee, a completed license agreement must be on file with Roger Wagner Publishing for commercial use of the HyperStudio Player.

Windows Compatible Stacks

HyperStudio stacks created on an Apple Macintosh computer are compatible with PCs running Windows and also the British Acorn computers. There are limitations to a stack's performance on these other computer platforms, however, simply because these three computing environments do not always share the same elements or support the same features. It is important to keep the stacks you wish to use between these computers simple, using only basic HyperStudio features when creating them, at this time. As future versions of HyperStudio are developed for these platforms, more compatibility will be built in to each version of the software. Knowledge about a PC running Windows or the British Acorn computer is helpful in sharing your stacks between these computers and the Macintosh. (Please see Chapter 10 on "HyperStudio and Windows")

Locking Stacks

There may be times (although we don't encourage it), when you may wish to limit the ability of a user to make changes to your stack, or how they move through your stack. This "locking" of a stack can take place several different ways. The possibilities are:

• Lock the file from the Finder.

• Hide the menu bars within your stack.

• Use the HyperStudio "lock" function.

Locking the stack file from the Finder is the best approach if what you want to prevent is changes to the stack file. Just go to the desktop, click once on the stack file, and then

---

Preferences

Stack preferences

Stack password: My Password
☐ Lock stack...
☐ Show card number with stack name
☐ Turn on Magic Buttons & HyperLinks
☐ Automatically save stack
☐ Presentation mode...
☐ Ignore extra mouse clicks

Program preferences
☒ I'm an experienced HyperStudio user
E-mail address:

Cancel   OK

Learn more about Preferences in the Preferences section.

choose "Get Info" from the File menu. An information box will appear, and in the lower-left corner, you'll see a checkbox labeled "lock". If you check this, the file cannot be changed in any way until you uncheck the box.

This has the advantage of giving your stack user full access to your stack, but eliminates any concern over the original file ever being changed.

NETWORK USERS: Note that stacks that will be opened by multiple users at the same time *must* be locked. This is true of any Macintosh document, and is done to avoid the potential conflict of two users making different changes to the same file

If you just want to casually limit the user's access to HyperStudio's editing features, even just for cosmetic purposes, the simplest way is to just use Command-H to hide the menu bar on a given card. If you want to hide *all* the menu bars throughout a stack, use Menu Tamer, which is described later in this chapter.

There is a third level of "protection" which is available, and is found in the Preferences item in the Edit menu of HyperStudio. Locking a stack here shortens the stack menu bar to just the Apple, File, Edit and Move menus. The tools and other editing menus are no longer available.

To lock a stack, choose Preferences from the Edit menu and check the "Lock Stack" box. Locking a stack allows you to restrict access to your stack. When you lock your stack, all of the menus will be removed from the menu except for File, Edit, and Move. The File menu will only allow the user to start a new stack, open a stack, save a stack, Print to Video, or quit. The Edit menu will only have the standard editing options ("Undo," "Cut," "Copy," "Paste," and "Clear") and "Preferences". Finally, the Move menu will contain only the standard stack navigation commands ("Back," "Home," "First," "Previous," "Next," "Last" and "Jump to Card..."), plus "Find Text..." Unlocking the stack restores the complete menu bar. Since this option is available via the Preferences dialog box, you may wish to set a password in Preferences so that users can't get to the "Lock stack" check box without knowing the password.

Note that there are some "context" features to locked stacks and whether the user can navigate through the stack manually. If the menu bar is visible in a locked stack, then the Move keyboard commands will be available. On the other hand, if the stack is locked *and* the menu bar is hidden, then the keyboard Move commands are no longer available. This gives the maxium control over just where, and in what order a stack user can visit the different cards.

As supporters of open learning, exploration, and sharing, we ask that you please use the locked stack and password features only where absolutely necessary. It's a bit frustrating to get a really neat stack from someone, and not be able to explore it to see how they did their work! We all learn from others, so share your talents openly!

Hiding the Menu Bar

Choosing "Hide Menu Bar" under the Options menu will hide the menu bar on a single card. If the menu bar is hidden when you quit HyperStudio, it will also be hidden when the user views that card provided your stack is saved with the menu bar hidden. This allows you to create stacks without a menu bar. Press Command-M to restore (or hide) the menu bar.

Menu Tamer Extra

Menu Tamer is an Extra found under the Extras menu and will hide or show the menu bar on all cards in the current stack, except for the card you are currently on. After selecting "Menu Tamer", you will be asked if you want to hide all of the menu bars or show all of them.

MenuChooser NBA

With this New Button Action you can access menu items at the click of a button! When creating a Button or Object Action, load the MenuChooser NBA by clicking "Disk Library" in the New Button Actions window. Locate the MenuChooser NBA and click "Use this NBA". Type the menu name followed by a comma and the menu item you'd like to use will be called up when you click on your Button or Object.

Items can also be identified by their number position in a menu, which is generally *not* convenient. However, it works out very well if you want to choose something from the Tools or Colors menus! For example, "Tools,7" would activate the rectangular selector tool!

For the hierarchal menus, such as the Ready Made cards, just just the last two items. For example, using "Ready Made Cards, Same bBackground" would create a new card with the same graphic background as the current card. This could actually be very useful to be able to have a button in one of your stacks that automatically added new cards from the Ready Made Card template list!

HideCursor NBA

When creating a Button or Object Action, load the HideCursor NBA by clicking "Disk Library" in the New Button Actions window. Locate the HideCursor NBA and click "Use this NBA". By typing "H", "S", or "O" in the window you can Hide the cursor, Show the cursor, or Obscure it. Obscure means that the cursor will be hidden until the mouse is moved.

Storyboard Extra

This Extra found under the Extras menu, will display all the cards in your stack, and let you rearrange the order, or delete cards as you wish. Once you choose this Extra, you will see a display with miniature-sized cards of your stack. From this window you can

The StoryBoard extra lets you sort, delete, even move to different cards within the current stack.

▼▼▼

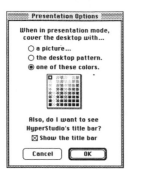

▲▲▲
The Presentation mode options dialog.

view your stack, delete cards and move them.

To delete a card simply click on it and once it is outlined in red, you can click on the "delete" button. To delete more than one card, press the Command key as you click on the cards you want to delete.

To move a card to a new position, simply click on the card and drag it between two other cards, or to its new position. To move more than one card at a time, press the shift key as you select the cards to be moved. The cards which will be moved will be outlined in red.

Presentation Mode

When this check box is checked in "Preferences" under the Edit menu, only your stack will show on the monitor desktop, regardless of the monitor size. After choosing "Presentation Mode", a dialog box will appear asking you to choose whether you'd like the desktop covered with a solid color, desktop pattern, or a graphic.

You will also be asked if you'd like the title bar of the stack to be hidden.

Once you've chosen a style, the card frame will be centered on the screen, and the desktop will be hidden.

Once the Presentation Mode is turned on, moving to other stacks, regardless of their Presentation Mode setting, will leave the frame image in view. Stacks saved while in Presentation Mode will acquire the current frame image. The frame image uses the same color palette as the card you are viewing, so frame colors may change from card to card if the color palettes are different.

Stack Actions

In HyperStudio, "buttons" are the most common way to trigger an action, but there are other ways as well! Not only can other objects such as graphic objects act like buttons,

▲▲▲
You can assign actions to the stack!

you can also elect to have your stack perform an action when it is first opened, when the stack is exited, or even any time that the user clicks the mouse somewhere in the stack that is not a "button"!

To access Stack Actions, go to the Objects menu and select "About this Stack...". You will see the "About Stack" window where information and choices about the stack may be made.

In each case you can use the "Things to Do" part of the usual HyperStudio Actions dialog box to Play a sound, Play a Movie or Video, Play animation, Use HyperLogo, New Button Actions, or use the Testing Functions. As the names indicate, these actions will be done when the stack is opened, exited, or when the user clicks the mouse anywhere within the stack, but not on a part of the card that would otherwise respond (such as another button, text field scroll bar, etc.)

Interactive Cursors

As the user moves through a stack, the usual cursor for the mouse is the "browse" cursor: the hand. However, HyperStudio also lets you specify special cursors when the mouse is over buttons, graphic objects, and other interactive elements of your stack.

As it happens, you can also choose an alternative cursor to the browse cursor if you wish. To choose an alternate cursor for your entire stack, locate the "Cursors" pop-up menu (it usually reads "None"), and and select a new cursor. Your cursor will change back to the default browse cursor when you move to another stack.

We suggest that you use the special interactive cursors sparingly. They can give the user extra feedback, such as in a game where you want the user to realize that they can click at the edges of the screen to move in that direction. On the other hand, non-intuitive use of the cursors can confuse the user.

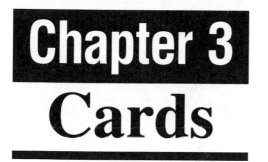
Chapter 3
Cards

A *card* is one of HyperStudio's most basic elements. Each individual *screen* within a stack is called a card. Every card within a stack will have, at a minimum, a background (see Chapter 5 on Graphics) and at least one or more objects—Text Objects, Graphic Objects, and so on. The number of cards a given stack can hold depends on available memory (RAM) and available hard disk space. In addition, a card can also have *actions* assigned to it. These actions can take place when the user first arrives at the card, exits, or clicks anywhere other than where there is a button or other interactive element (such a scrolling text field).

Adding A New Card

Adding a new card to your stack is easy! Just choose *New Card* in the **Edit** menu (or type Command-N). The card will be added without any objects and the background will made the current background color.

Any new card you make will be created directly after the card you are on. For example, if you are on card 3 and create a new card, your new card will become card number 4. Any cards at position 4 and beyond simply "slide over" to higher positions to accomodate the new card. What was card number 4 would then be at position 5, followed by whatever other cards were in the stack at the time New Card was chosen.

If you want to add a new card at the "end" of your current stack always remember to move to the last card of stack (Command-9, or use the Move menu).

If you want to add a card at the very beginning of your stack, it's a little bit trickier... and very easy! Just create a new card anywhere in your stack, and then choose "Title Card" from the Extras menu. That will move whatever card you are currently looking at to the first position in your stack!

```
Edit
 Undo              ⌘Z

 Cut               ⌘H
 Copy              ⌘C
 Paste             ⌘U
 Clear

 New Card          ⌘N
 Ready Made Cards  ▶   Blank Card
 Delete Card           Same Background
 Cut Card              Group Card
 Copy Card

 Edit this Object...

 Effects           ▶
 Erase Background...

 Preferences       ⌘;
```

▲▲▲

Using *Ready Made Cards* for adding a new card.

Cards can also be "pasted" into whatever position you are currently at in a stack. Obviously, you'll need to cut or copy them from other positions in the same stack (or even other stacks) before you choose Paste Card from the Edit menu.

Ready Made Cards

Another method for adding a new card is by using *Ready Made Cards* in the **Edit** menu. Ready Made Cards gives you four options for adding a new card:

1. Blank card: This creates a card just as if you used the *New Card* command.

2. Same Background: This creates a card with the background image the same as the current card you're on. (See also *Chapter 5, Graphics* for more information on background images.)

3. Group Card: This creates a card that becomes a part of a group associated with the current card you're on. (See also *Group Card* later in this chapter.)

4. Ready Made Cards folder: Sort of like clip-art, HyperStudio also offers "clip-cards"! Below the first three choices in the Ready Made Cards list is a custom list of pre-made cards that can be inserted in your stack any time you wish. The cards can contain not only art, but pre-arranged text objects, buttons with actions, or any other elements you wish. The items you see there now are samples that we have provided, but the list can be customized with your own card templates as well. This might be handy if you use the same card style often.

To add your own Ready Made Cards to the list, Create one card stacks of the templates you'd like to have available, and save them in the Ready Made Cards folder within your HyperStudio folder. The next time you restart HyperStudio, your Ready Made card will be in the menu!

Deleting a Card

Cards are easily deleted using the Edit menu. You can choose "Delete Card" to permanently remove a card, or, you can choose "Cut Card" if you wish to move the card to another position in your stack or to a completely different stack.

"Delete Card" does not require as much available free memory as "Cut Card", since nothing is kept on the clipboard.

Cards that are cut remain on the clipboard until your next cut or copy operation, or until you Quit HyperStudio. Remember that putting an entire card, with graphics, sounds, etc. will take as much memory as the card itself occupies, so this may present a problem for cards that use a lot of memory in a stack that is also very large.

If you want to delete a range of cards, or just number of them from different places in your stack, the easiest way is to use the Storyboard, found in the Extras menu. See the description of the Storyboard in Chapter 2 on Stacks.

Copying and Moving Cards

Cards can be easily moved from one place to another. Within a stack, you can always choose "Cut Card" with the desired card in view, then move to the card in your stack that you would like the card on the clipboard pasted *after*. When you click "Paste", your card will come into view. Remember that your card is still on the clipboard, so if for some reason you'd like to paste additional copies of the card, simply choose "Paste Card" again.

An alternative way of moving cards is to use the Storyboard Extra. This gives you a graphic overview of your entire stack, and lets you use the mouse to drag cards to whatever new positions you'd like.

If you should have a problem moving a large card to another stack, one approach would be to *temporarily* delete other cards in the stack, then do the "Copy". Then move to the destination stack and do the paste, *without* saving the changes to the first stack. Finally, return to the first stack and actually delete the card that was moved. If you just want to move a large card within a stack, the Storyboard Extra can directly move a card, without requiring the additional memory that a copy/paste operation would require.

Moving Between Cards

You can move between cards by going to the Move menu or by creating Buttons that take you from one card to another. The keyboard commands found under the Move menu are a quick way to move from one card to another.

Cards in a stack "wrap-around". That is, selecting "Next card" under the Move menu when you are on the last card in a stack brings you to the first card. Similarly, if you are on the first card of your stack, and choose "Previous Card", you'll "wrap-around" to the last card!

Changing the Size of a Card

You can change the size of the card you'd like to work with, by choosing *About this Stack...* from the **Objects** menu. Click on the Change # of colors or size button to choose different card sizes.

Note that all cards within the stack will be changed to the new size. HyperStudio will automatically "adjust" all graphics, including the background image, along with objects, to fit the new size. *Use this feature with caution!*

▲▲▲
The Stack Information dialog.

The About Card dialog

▼▼▼

```
≡≡≡≡≡≡≡≡≡  About Card - 1  ≡≡≡≡≡≡≡≡≡
 ┌────────────────────────────────────┐
 │ Card name: [Sample]      Card ID:  1 │
 │                                      │
 │ The entire card uses: 2 K   The background uses: 2 K │
 │ ┌ Things to do when: ─┐ ┌ Card settings: ─┐ │
 │ │ ☐ arriving at this card... │ │ ☐ Lock colors │ │
 │ │ ☐ leaving this card...     │ │ ☐ Group card  │ │
 │ │ ☐ clicking on this card... │ │ ☐ Marked card │ │
 │                                      │
 │  Cursor:  [ 🖑 ▼]   ( Cancel )  ( OK ) │
 └────────────────────────────────────┘
```

Card Features

By choosing "About This Card" from the Objects menu, you can find out quite a bit of information about that particular card in your stack, and also set up some additional features. These include:

Card ID and Name

Each card within a stack has a unique **ID** (identification) number. An ID is assigned to the card automatically by HyperStudio when the card is first created. Note that the card ID number *is not* the same as a card's *position* in the stack—it will remain the same, regardless of the actual postion of the card. The ID number is mainly of use to HyperLogo and some NBAs.

Giving a card a **name** is useful for easily identifying individual cards. For example, when using the *Jump To Card...* command in the **Move** menu, you can use a card's name to immediately jump to that particular card. Also, the Storyboard Extra will display the names of the cards in your stack, making it easier for you to identify individual cards as you work with them there..

Lock colors

The "Import Background" command brings in custom colors as well as an image. Checking this item will "freeze" the current color set for the card, even if you then import a new background graphic. This is mostly useful when you ultimately want the color set of a particular piece of clip-art, but intend to actually load a different background graphic. See Chapter 5 on Graphics for more information.

Marked card

A Marked card is "tagged" so that a button using the **Places To Go** action *Last marked card* will move the user to the last marked card they visited, even if it was in different stack.

Group Card

This will designate this particular card to be a part of a group. Group cards have the advantage of being able to share backgrounds and group objects. A new card can be made a part of the group by using **Edit** menu: *Ready Made Cards—Group card*. A group card can be ungrouped by unchecking this option.

Card Cursor

A card normally has the browse cursor. However, you can give each card its own cursor by using this option. When a card is displayed, the cursor will change to the cursor you've assigned for that particular card. If no cursor is specified, it will default back to the browse cursor, unless a stack cursor has also been defined.

Card Information

The entire card uses:

This tells you how much memory the card uses in your stack.

The background uses:

This tells you how much memory the background image of that particular card uses in your stack.

Card Actions

As was discussed with Stack Actions, not only can buttons trigger actions, but so can clicking on other objects. In addition, you can set up an action that you'd like to take place when the user first arrives at, or exits a particular card. For example, if you wanted a voice prompt, or a QuickTime or laserdisc movie to play as soon as the card first appeared, setting up a "Card Action" would be one way to do it. (The other way would be by creating an "Automatic Timer" button. See the chapter on buttons for more information on that approach).

You can also set up an effect that will happen whenever the user clicks the

The *Actions* dialog for *arriving at* and *leaving* a card.
▼▼▼

```
┌─────────────────────────────┐
│▒▒▒▒▒▒▒▒ Actions ▒▒▒▒▒▒▒▒▒│
├─────────────────────────────┤
│ ┌─ Things To Do: ──────────┐│
│ │ □ Play a sound...        ││
│ │ □ Play a Movie or Video...││
│ │ □ New Button Actions...  ││
│ │ □ Play animation...      ││
│ │ □ Use HyperLogo...       ││
│ │ □ Testing functions...   ││
│ └──────────────────────────┘│
│                             │
│  ( Cancel )  ( Done  )     │
└─────────────────────────────┘
```

mouse somewhere in the stack that is not a "button"! For example, if you wanted to quickly set up a "corrective" prompt, such as the phrase "Click on one of the menu items.", setting up a Card Action assigned to "Clicking on this Card" would do the trick. Alternatively, you could create a large, invisible button the size of the card that would be "behind" all the other buttons and objects on the card.

This is mentioned so as to point out that many times there are several different ways of accomplishing the same ultimate result in your stack. Which approach is "best" depends on your own preferences and objectives for that project.

To access Card Actions, go to the Objects menu and select "About this Stack...". You will see the "About Stack" window where the "Actions" button can be clicked to go to the Card Actions dialog box..

There you can use the "Things to Do" part of the usual HyperStudio Actions dialog box to Play a sound, Play a Movie or Video, Play animation, Use HyperLogo, New Button Actions,or use the Testing Functions. As the names indicate, these actions will be done when the stack is opened, exited, or when the user clicks the mouse anywhere within the stack, but not on a part of the card that would otherwise respond (such as another button, text field scroll bar, etc.)

Arranging Cards

Title Card Extra

This Extra found under the **Extras** menu moves the current card, regardless of its current position, to the beginning of your stack and makes it card number 1.

The Storyboard Extra

▼▼▼

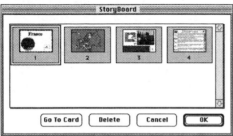

Storyboard Extra

This Extra found under the **Extras** menu will display all the cards in your stack, and let you rearrange the order, or delete cards as you wish. Once you choose this extra, you will see a display with miniature-sized cards of your stack. From this window you can view your stack, delete cards and move them.

To delete a card click on it once (it becomes outlined in red), then click on the "delete" button. To delete more than one card at a time, press the shift key as you click on the cards you want to delete.

To move a card to a new position, click on the card and drag it between two other cards, or to its new position. To move more than one card at a time, press the shift key as you select the cards to be moved. The cards to be moved will be outlined in red.

Chapter 4
Buttons

Buttons are the basic way that most stacks let the user control their movement through the stack, the activation of multimedia elements like sound, video and animation, and other actions as well. Although other objects can act like buttons (such as graphic objects), true buttons are probably what you'll use the most often.

Adding a Button

Selecting *Add a Button...* from the **Objects** menu allows you to add a button to the current card. In essence, there are just two things HyperStudio needs to know: what do you want your button to look like on the card, and what should it do when the user clicks on it. These are the things that the next set of steps determine.

Button Appearance

After choosing Add a Button, you'll be presented with the "Button Appearance" dialog box. Once the button has been placed on the card, you will be presented with the Actions dialog. Let's look at each of the areas of the Button Appearance dialog:

Button Types

There are eight different types of buttons that you may define in HyperStudio. The first four are visible and automatically highlight when clicked, and the remaining four are invisible and will highlight when clicked only if you have the "Highlight" Check box marked. (This is automatic if you haven't checked "Experienced User" in Preferences).

Rounded Rectangle

The Rounded Rectangle button is the default. It simply looks like a rectangle with rounded corners.

The Button Appearance dialog lets you choose how your button will look before it's placed on the card.

▼▼▼

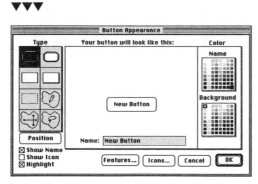

Rounded Double Rectangle

The rounded rectangle button has a special attribute. This button can be activated by pressing the Return or Enter key on your keyboard!

Rectangle

The Rectangle button is also a very simple button.

Drop Shadow Rectangle

This button has a shadow behind it to give it more visual depth on the card.

Freehand Area Button

This button type allows you to draw the shape of your button. After selecting this button type and clicking "Position...", you are presented with your card and a pencil cursor. Draw the button's shape using the pencil cursor.

Expanding Area Button

This button type allows you to specify the inside of your button area, and it will determine the appropriate edges. After selecting this button type and clicking "Position...", you are presented with your card and a four-headed arrow cursor. Click inside the boundary of a closed, solid color area on the background image. HyperStudio will work out from that point to find the edges for the button. (This is very useful when you have a map, for example. You can click in the center of a region, and HyperStudio will go out from that point to find the proper border.)

Lasso Area Button

This button type is the opposite of the Expanding Area Button, above: it allows you to lasso an object on the screen, and HyperStudio will hug up against the object to define the button's shape. The button name or any icon associated with the button will show up on the button if you check the "Show Name" and/or "Show Icon" Check boxes. After selecting this button type and clicking "Position...", you are presented with your card and a lasso cursor. Simply use the lasso and draw around the object that will define the button's shape. If the object is on a solid background, you don't need to drag neatly; the lasso will contract and shrink down to find the edges of the object.

Button Options

The series of checkboxes just below the button styles are provided to let you determine whether you want the name of your button visible, whether you'd like to have a small graphic called an "icon" as part of your button, and whether you want the button to highlight when the user clicks on it.

Show Name

Marking this Check box makes the button name visible—whatever is typed into the name box will be shown inside the button in 12-point Chicago in whatever color is selected in the "Name" color selection menu. Button names that describe an action ("Next Card", "Cancel", "Launch BongoWorks") can help the user. Button names can stand for the response from the user ("True", "1492", "All the above"). You do not have to name the button, although it may be useful. Scripts and stacks that use the test functions may refer to the button's name.

If "Show Name" is checked, the button name will appear in whatever color is selected in the "Name" color selection menu. The rest of the button will be the color chosen in the "Background" color selection menu.

Show Icon

If an icon has already been set up for a button, unchecking this will remove the icon from the button. On the other hand, if an icon has not yet been assigned to the button, checking "Show Icon" is the same as clicking the "Icons..." button at the bottom of the Button Appearance dialog. Either approach opens the "Icon Info"

▲▲▲
You can select an icon from the samples library, or choose one from disk!

The Button Features dialog.
▼▼▼

dialog. In this dialog box, you can select an icon that will appear on the button

When the icon display appears, what you see is a sample selection of popular button icons. To select an icon, simply click it, and then click on "Ok" to go back to the Button Appearance dialog.

If you would like to see what icons are already in use within the stack, you can click "In Use".

Clicking "Disk Library..." will bring up the Standard File dialog, and show you any icon files that you may have on your disk. The HS Art folder in your HyperStudio folder has additional button icons that you may find useful.

NOTE: If you've checked "Experienced User" in the Preferences, HyperStudio will display all files in the file selection dialog box. This allows you to open any file that may have embedded icons. After opening that file, if the file contains any icons, HyperStudio will display them, at which point you can select what yo wish to use.

Highlight

If you would like your invisible buttons to "blink" when clicked, check the "Highlight" box. Visible buttons are automatically highlighted.

Button Features

If you've checked "Experienced User" in preferences, you'll see a choice labeled "Features..." at the bottom of the Button Appearance dialog. Clicking it opens the Item Features window. This dialog box is divided into two halves.

The upper portion tells you the type of item (in this case a button), the amount of memory it occupies (including all attached items such as sounds, animations, or script), the "owner" card (where the button is part of a group), the button's ID, and the button's position on the card. The button's ID and position can be useful for certain HyperLogo commands, which require either a button's ID number or name.

The lower portion of the Item Features window shows 5 Check boxes.

Locked

With this box checked, the button may not be moved or edited.

Group Item

Any button with this item checked will show up on all cards within the same group. If you unmark this Check box, the button will no longer be a group item and will appear only on the card you were at when you unchecked this box. Marking the box will cause the button to once again be shared with all of the cards in the group.

Drop off only

A button which is "Drop off only" will be activated only when a draggable Graphic Object is dropped onto it. Clicking the button with the Browse tool will have no effect.

Hidden

When the "Hidden" Check box is marked, the entire button is invisible and may not be clicked. Automatic timer, when hidden will remain inactive (It will show up, however, when you switch to the Edit tool or Button tool.).

No Click

When the "No Click" Check box is marked, the button can be activated by simply passing the mouse across the button without actually clicking!

Button Cursor

Note, at the bottom of the Item Features window there is an item labeled "None". This is the current alternate cursor for that button. Holding the mouse button down on "None" will let you choose an alternate cursor for this button. When passing the mouse over that button, the browse cursor will change to the new cursor.

Button Actions

After you've decided what your button should look like, and placed it on the screen, the next step is to choose what you'd like to have happen when someone clicks on the button!

Play a Sound

You can have a sound play when a button is clicked. If you choose this Action when making a Button, you will see the Tape Deck window. It will allow you to select an existing sound or record a new one.

Use HyperLogo...

You may choose this Action when making a Button. HyperLogo is a scripting language for HyperStudio that is documented in a separate manual. Please see the HyperLogo Reference Manual for information on this feature.

Animation

A button can play an animation. Please see the section on animation to learn how either "path" or "cel" animations may be played when clicking on a button.

Automatic timer

Normally, a button must be clicked to be activated. A Magic Button activates automatically (as if someone had clicked it) after a specified number of seconds. The button can also be set to continuously cycle.

Automatic timers work well for a help system; a help card or item could be displayed if they user doesn't click something on a card in a certain amount of time, for example. Automatic timer can also be used to create timed tests.

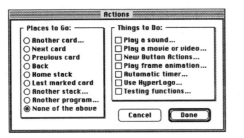

▲▲▲
Here's where all the action is! The Actions window lets you choose what your button will do.

Note that automatic timer are not active until you turn on the automatic timer function in the Preferences dialog box, and you are in the Browse mode. This way, buttons won't be activating while you're using an Edit or Paint tool and trying to work on your stack. If Automatic timer are not turned on in the Preferences dialog box, you will be asked if you'd like them turned on at this time.

A series of automatic timed buttons can be used to "orchestrate" a sequence on a card. For example, you could use one magic button to play a sound (after one second), then a second magic button to start an automation after three seconds, followed several seconds later (via a third magic button) with another sound.

Choices when selecting Automatic timer... are:

Activate button as soon as card is shown

The button will be triggered immediately upon arrival at that card.

Activate button after card is shown

Activate after ____ seconds: Enter a time (in seconds) after which the button should activate.

Repeating

The "Repeating" Check box will activate the button again and again.

New Button Actions...

Although the HyperStudio Button Action menu provides the actions that you'll most commonly need for a button, there's always room for improvement! HyperStudio provides for additional button actions through an option named, appropriately enough, "New Button Actions", or "NBAs" for short.

Clicking the "New Button Actions..." check box in the Actions dialog will bring up the New Button Actions dialog. In the upper-left corner of this dialog is a list of some of the more popular NBAs, built into HyperStudio.

As with the icon selection process, if you'd like to see a list of NBAs already in use in the stack, you can click on the "**In Use**" button at the bottom of the screen.

The New Button Actions (NBA) dialog.
▼▼▼

New Button Actions

Names:	Info:
HideShow	Animator™
RollCredits	by Steven Allen
CDPlay	Macintosh version 2.50 by Ken Kashmarek
Animator	This NBA makes creating animation fun and easy!

Use this NBA...   Cancel
○ Samples ○ In Use ● Disk Library...   OK

Clicking on "**Disk Library**" will let you select additional NBAs from the "NBAs & Extras" folder in your HyperStudio folder. Even more are located in the "More NBAs" folder in the HS Utilities folder on the HyperStudio System CD-ROM.

Immediately to the right of the list of NBAs is a help box, with instructions for the currently selected NBA. It will normally contain information on the name of the NBA, the author, and information on how to use it. If you would like to use the NBA, click the "Use NBA..." button at the bottom of the screen. If the NBA needs any additional information from you, it will prompt you as appropriate. (For example, an NBA that hides a Text Object will ask you for the name of the Text Object to hide.)

There are NBAs that are useful in dealing with buttons. Here are a few of them:

Button Runner NBA

By typing in the names of buttons (one per line), HyperStudio will execute their actions in that order. A really neat feature is that the buttons do not have to be on the current card.

HideShow NBA

This NBA allows you to hide or show a Graphic Object, a Button, or a Text Object. You can achieve impressive "special effects" by pre-hiding graphic objects, then showing them at the click of a button. Possibilities include fake dialog boxes, "pop-up menus" and more.

To use the HideShow NBA, simply select it from the sample in the New Button Actions... window when creating a button and then click "Use this NBA". You will be prompted for three things: Type the name of the object you wish to work with, (If you have only one Text Object, Graphic Object or Button on the card, you do not have to enter the object name to be shown, hidden or flipped.).

▲▲▲
The HideShow NBA dialog.

Check the type of object, and whether you want to hide it, show it, or flip it (that is hide it if it's visible, or show it if it's already hidden.).

Changing the Sample NBAs

When "Samples" is selected at the bottom of the NBA dialog, you'll see a list of popular NBAs. Although you can always load other NBAs from disk, you can also change the list of NBAs offered in the Samples list. The NBAs in the Samples list are all part of a stack in your HyperStudio folder named "HS Samples Library". If you load this stack, and add or delete buttons that have NBAs attached to them, then the corresponding NBAs will be the ones that come up in the Samples list when you are using HyperStudio with any other stack.

Testing Functions

HyperStudio's main purpose is for individually created projects, not for the making of electronic multiple choice tests. However, HyperStudio's "testing function" can be useful for gathering information as a user goes through your stack. This information can take the form of a simple test.

HyperStudio's testing functions allow you to create a stack which keeps track of buttons that have been clicked, and stores the results in a text file on disk. Buttons may have one of four test effects: "No Testing Function," "Correct Answer," "Ask User Name," or "Alternate Answer." Normally the setting is "No Testing Function," and buttons created this way are neutral. That is, they have no effect on the test status of a stack or card.

No Testing Function

This is the default value for a button, and causes no test effects to happen. HyperStudio will not record if this button is clicked.

Correct Answer

This causes the button to add 1 to the total score.

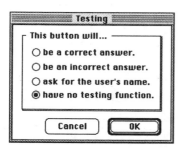

▲▲▲
There are several options when using the testing features in HyperStudio, as show here in the Testing feature dialog.

Incorrect Answer

Clicking this button does not add to the total score.

Ask User Name

When this option is marked for a button, the user is prompted to type in their own name. This does not change the button name. The user's name is stored in the HS.Test.Results file.

If you choose to make any button in a stack either "Correct Answer" or "Incorrect Answer," that stack is considered a "test stack."

When a test stack is exited (by launching another application, branching to another stack, or simply quitting HyperStudio), HyperStudio scans the entire stack to see what buttons were pressed as the stack was being used. HyperStudio writes to a text file in the same folder as the stack, named HS.Test.Results.

The information written in this text file includes the stack name, the time and date, a list of which buttons were chosen on each card, and a final "score" for that stack. Information is written to the HS.Test.Results file on a cumulative basis, so this file contains the results of all stacks in that folder that are used until the file HS.Test.Results is deleted. The HS.Test.Results file is written to only if there are test effect buttons in the stack.

If no button on that card was clicked, or if the button clicked had "No test effect" (the default), then no entry is written for that card.

If a button on the card defined as either "Correct Answer" or "Incorrect Answer" is clicked, HyperStudio will record the button name as the chosen button for that card.

There can be as many "Correct Answer," "Incorrect Answer," or "No test effect" buttons on a card as you want; only the most recently pressed button with a "Correct

Answer" or "Incorrect Answer" function will be counted.

You may want to experiment with different button combinations to see what works best for you. Possible options include:

- Each card contains one question. Each possible answer button *also* moves the user to the next card. The "Correct Answer" test effect is used for the right answer on each card; the remaining buttons are set for "Incorrect Answer".

- Include forward and backward arrow buttons on each card. Define them as "No test effect." Clicking these will not affect the "last button clicked" status on a card, so the user could click a choice, and then change their mind and choose a different choice. When they finally click the forward button, HyperStudio would still record the test effect button chosen.

- A timed test: Each screen includes an Auto Timed (no test effect) button that moves to the next card after 25 seconds (for example). The user would have to choose one of the answer buttons before the time is up. The final HS.Test.Results file would record which button on each card had been chosen.

Even if it's not a multiple-choice graded test that you're creating, there are other data-collection projects that will find the "testing function" a helpful option. For example, you could create a stack to survey people's opinions. Imagine a stack that has a card with a picture of three bowls of ice cream. Each bowl has an invisible button over it, named "chocolate," "vanilla," and "strawberry" (respectively). When the stack terminates, the HS.Test.Results file tells you which button was selected. In this case, the "Correct" or "Incorrect" attribute for a button doesn't matter (though it must be one or the other): what you're getting is the information about which item the users chose. If 100 people used this stack, the HS.Test.Results file will contain a survey of 100 people—a study of the percentage of which flavor ice cream was preferred.

Reference

TIP

- To use the test results, load the HS.Test.Results file into a word processor or disk-based Text Object.

- The HyperLogo Tutorial shows how to create testing stacks with HyperLogo, rather than the automated test function. This has the advantage that you don't need to leave the stack to create the test results, nor do you need to read the file from disk to do the analysis. If you do want to use HyperLogo to open and analyze the HS.Test.Results file, see the Testing Stack example in the HyperLogo sample stacks.

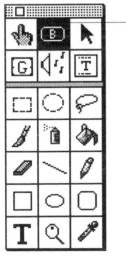

▲▲▲

To edit a button (copy, move, etc.) select the Button Editor tool from the Tools menu. You can also use the Arrow tool as well.

Here's a sample of the HS.Test.Results file, after running a stack with 5 questions.

```
name of test stackTest.Stack
name of studentTerry McConnell
date and time10/14/94 4:10:42 AM
card ID (not position)3
name of button with answerMickey
card ID4
name of button with answerDonald
card ID7
name of button with answerGoofy
card ID2
name of button with answerPluto
card ID6
name of button with answerW. Elias Disney
SCORE
correct answers3
total answers4
-END-
```

Cutting, Copying & Pasting Buttons

Buttons can be cut or copied from one card or stack and pasted onto another card or into another stack with all the functions that were attached to the button "still there".

To do this, you need to click on the Button Edit tool which is in the Tool Box (Invisible Buttons will become visible). Now, click on the button on your card you wish to copy. Choose "Copy button" from the Edit menu. Move to the card or a card in another stack you wish to paste the button on and choose "Paste button" from the Edit menu. Select the Browse tool from the Tool Box to use your button. Buttons can also be cut from the card, or simply deleted by first selecting the button, and then pressing the Delete key (or choose Clear from the Edit menu).

Graphics

Backgrounds, Clip Art, Paint Tools & Graphic Objects

If a word processor is an environment where the main form is a page with words, to which graphics can be added, then multimedia is very much like a paint program on which text boxes and buttons are the "additions". Perhaps that's why HyperStudio is so easy to use: if you know how to use a computer paint program of even the simplest kind, then you already know the basics of the HyperStudio environment.

There are a number of ways to use graphics in HyperStudio—Backgrounds, Clip Art, Paint Tools & Graphic Objects. This chapter explores each of these. Before we begin, however, there are a few fundamentals which will help you understand the differences:

Backgrounds

Whenever you use the paint tools or add clip art, you are working on what's called the "background". Every card in a stack has a background image; even those with just a solid color. Objects—Buttons, Graphic Objects and Text Objects—are placed in front of the background; the background is simply a static image on which the objects are presented.

Paint Tools

With HyperStudio's paint tools you can create your own art, modify the background, and even save your own created graphic images to disk for later use.

Clip Art

To add a small graphic image to the background, without changing the entire background image, you would use a piece of *clip art*. Clip art allows you to choose a *portion* of a graphic image, as opposed to the entire graphic image. Once a piece of clip art is added, it becomes a part of the overall background image.

Graphic Objects

These are objects that "float" in front of the background. Graphic objects retain their own identity as an object on the card. This is in contrast to adding clip art, whereas Graphic Objects do not become a part of the background image. In addition, you can also assign *actions* to Graphic Objects, just as you can with Buttons, for example.

Graphic File Formats Supported

HyperStudio supports a number of standard graphic file formats. You can use any PICT, TIFF, EPS, JPEG, PCX, BMP, GIF, MacPaint, Photo-CD, or any standard Apple IIGs picture. In addition, you can use images from a video digitizer and photographs can be used as graphics directly from a QuickTake camera, as explained next.

Graphic Image Sources

HyperStudio provides several ways for obtaining graphic images. Whether you are adding clip art, importing a background or adding a Graphic Object, the choices of *where* the graphic image *comes from* are the same.

Normally you add graphic images from a file on your hard drive. However, if you have either a video digitizer or a QuickTake camera connected to your computer, you will be presented with the *Video Source* dialog This dialog allows you to select from either **Disk file**, **Video**, or **QuickTake camera** as the source of the graphic image. *If you do not have either a video digitizer or a QuickTake camera, you will not see the Video Source dialog. In that case you will be selecting graphic images from a disk file, as explained below.*

The choices for adding graphic images are:

Disk File

This adds a graphic image from your hard drive, floppy disk, or CD-ROM disk. This

If you have a video digitizer or QuickTake camera connected to your computer, you will have the option of selecting the *source* of the graphic image.

▼▼▼

Where do you want to get your picture from?
- ● Disk file
- ○ Video
- ○ QuickTake camera

[Cancel] [OK]

▲▲▲
The Video Digitizer window

method uses the standard file dialog which displays graphic image files that are supported by HyperStudio (See *Graphic File Formats Supported*, above).

This is the default method for obtaining graphic images if you do not have a video digitizer or QuickTake camera connected to your computer.

Video

If you have a video digitizer connected to your computer you can instantly digitize images from any external video source—such as a camcorder, for example.

Using this method will present the *Video Digitizer* window. Click on the **Options** button to make adjustments to your live image or the **Freeze** button to capture a still picture. Click **OK** to capture the image.

QuickTake Camera

If you have a QuickTake camera connected to your computer, you can use the QuickTake images without having to exit HyperStudio. You will see "slides" of the pictures. Choose the slide you want by double clicking on it.

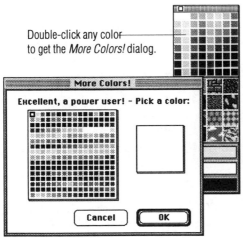

▲▲▲
Double-clicking a color in the Color palette brings up the *More Colors!* dialog.

Working With Colors

HyperStudio supports a variety of color *depths* (color depth is the number of different colors available in the **Color** menu). You can determine the amount of colors a stack uses by selecting from the **Objects** menu: *About this stack...*, where you can choose between a 2, 16 or 256-color stack.

Choosing A New Color

Double-clicking on any of the colors in the 256-color palette will take you to the *More Colors!* window where you can choose a new color to replace the one you clicked on.

Double-clicking on a color in the *More Colors!* window, will display the Apple system color selector where you can create a custom color! These color changes can only be made if you have *I am an experienced HyperStudio user* checked in the **Edit** menu: *Preferences* dialog.

Replacing Colors

This Replace Colors command in the *Effects*, **Edit** menu allows you to replace one color with another—in a selected area or over the entire background—or swap (exchange) two different colors. To use this option:

1. Select the area that you would like to change by using any of the selection tools— Rectangle Selector, Circle Selector or Lasso. *If you don't select anything, the entire background will be affected.*

2. Select *Replace Colors...* and choose the action that you would like to perform— replace or swap—and select the two colors from the palettes. Clicking **OK** will perform the action; if you don't like the results, choose *Undo* from the **Edit** menu.

Editing Graphics

There are a number of ways to edit graphic images such as copy, erase, move, rotate, scale and other such tasks. The following describes the various possibilities:

Copying and Pasting Graphics

Using a selector tool, select the area of the background image to be copied. Then select **Edit** menu: *Copy*. Move to the card you wish to "Paste" your graphic on. Go to the **Edit** menu and choose *Paste* to place a copy of your graphic in the desired location.

To copy and paste a Graphic Object, follow the above directions, only use the Graphic Edit tool or the Pointer to select the Graphic Object.

Deleting Graphics

To delete a painted area on your card, select the area of the background image you want to delete with a selector tool. Then choose **Edit** menu: *Clear* or *Cut*; or simply press the Delete key. You can also use the Eraser tool to erase a portion of the background image.

To delete a Graphic Object, select it with the Graphic Edit tool or the Pointer and press the Delete key.

Moving Graphics

To move a painted area on your card, select the area of the background image you want to move with a selector tool. While the flashing dots are active, move your mouse cursor to the center of the selected and drag it to its new location.

To move a Graphic Object, select it with the Graphic Edit tool or the Pointer and drag it to its new location.

Undo Painting

If you change your mind or make a mistake after using a paint tool, just choose from the **Edit** menu: *Undo*, or type ⌘-Z. You can only undo your most *recent* painting action—for example, if you draw three lines with the Line tool, then select **Edit**: *Undo*, only two lines will remain.

In the above example, selecting *Undo* a second time will bring the third line back again. It's kind of like *undoing* the *Undo!*

Special Effects With Graphics

The following special effects can be used for creating some interesting effects with graphic images. (Note: these are not for Graphic Objects, but painted graphic images appearing on the background of the card.)

Scale & Rotate

Using the Rectangle Selector tool, select a piece of clip art on the background. You can use "Flip Sideways", "Flip Upside Down" or "Scale and Rotate" from Effects under the Edit menu. Once you click away from the image, it will be "pasted" onto the background again and will no longer be selected.

Cookie Cutter Effect

Using the Lasso selection tool, hold down the Command key while selecting a graphic to do a "pencil lasso". Everywhere you move the mouse will be selected. Hold down the Option key while clicking inside a solid colored shape to do an "expanding lasso" selection. This will lasso the entire shape that corresponds to where you first click the mouse. You can simply lasso your shape or graphic to select it. After your graphic is selected, hold down the option key and "drag" a copy of your shape off of the original. You can drag off as many copies as you like. Now you have a cookie cutter!

Pictures From Other Sources

You can load pictures created with other paint programs that have custom colors, but you must be careful in using these graphics on a card. A custom color set may interfere with the appearance of the menu bar, or other buttons or graphics on the screen.

HyperStudio will match any imported clip art's color set to the card background's color set. Any time clip art with a different color set is imported, HyperStudio will match the colors on the imported art. This means that any time there are more or different colors in clip art than the current background, HyperStudio mixes the colors it has so that it can get as close to the original color as possible.

See also *Appendix B, Using HyperStudio with Other Programs.*

Backgrounds

A background is the "painting" that provides the backdrop for a card. It could look like the pages of a book, for example, or a background can be just a solid color. A stack can have as many different backgrounds as it has cards; or, it can have just one background, shared among all of the cards in the same stack.

The *Import Background...* command

▼▼▼

File
New Stack
Open Stack... ⌘O
Save Stack ⌘S
Save Stack As...
Import Background... ⌘I
Export Screen... ⌘E

Importing A Background

The *Import Background* command in the **File** menu loads a graphic image from any graphic image source (see *Graphic Image Sources*, earlier in this chapter). The imported graphic image will be used as the background for the *current* card.

When the graphic image is imported it will "fill" the entire background; thus, erasing anything that was there before—so be careful!

To import a background image:

1. Select **File** menu: *Import Background...*

2. Use the standard file dialog to select a graphic image file; or, select the source of the graphic image if you have a video digitizer or QuickTake camera.

3. If the image is larger or smaller than the size of the card, you will be asked if HyperStudio should re-size the image for you.

   • Choosing **Yes** will re-size the image to fit the card. *Some distortion may occur, depending on the size of both the image and the card.*

   • Choosing **No** will place the image in its original size and centered on the card. *If the image is larger than the card size, some cropping will occur.*

4. The graphic image will be imported and fill the background of the current card.

This dialog appears if the graphic image you are importing as a background is larger or smaller than the size of the card.

▼▼▼

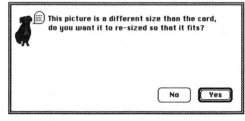

This picture is a different size than the card, do you want it to re-sized so that it fits?

[No] [**Yes**]

After you've imported a background image, you can modify it by using HyperStudio's paint tools or by adding clip art. You can also use almost any drawing or paint program to create your own backgrounds for use in your stacks.

Adding a card with the same background as the current card.

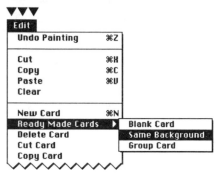

Adding a card that will share the same background as the current card.

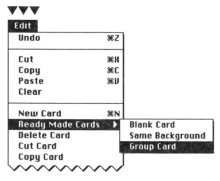

Copying A Background To A New Card

When adding a new card, you can have it use a copy of the current card's background.

1. Select from the **Edit** menu: *Ready Made Cards—Same Background.*

2. As the new card is created, it makes a *copy* of the current card's background and automatically uses it as its own background.

Modifying the background of the new card—by using the Paint tools, for example—will not affect or change the other card's background.

Sharing A Background Among Cards

There will be times when you want the same background to be "shared" by several cards. There are advantages to having cards share the same background:

- Since a background takes up a certain amount of memory and disk space, sharing a background among cards will help reduce the overall size of your stack.

- Making a change to the background on one card will affect all the cards that share that particular background. This saves you from having to repeat the same change on the other cards.

- Cards that share the same background can also share the same objects. When you add, delete or move a button, for example, it moves on all the cards in that group!

To add a card that shares the background of the current card:

1. Select from the **Edit** menu: *Ready Made Cards—Group Card.*

2. When the new card is added, it will use the same background as the current card. *This is not the same as "copying" a background as mentioned above—the new card will share the actual background of the other card.*

Changes to the background on one card will affect the background on all other cards *within that group*. For more information on group cards, refer to *Chapter 3, Cards*.

Clip Art

Clip art is a small "piece of art" used to enhance the background of a card. Using clip art provides a way for you to choose just a *portion* of a graphic image, as opposed to the *entire* graphic image. Once clip art has been added to your card, it becomes a part of the card's background image.

Note: Be careful not to confuse using clip art with adding a Graphic Object. The latter does not become a part of the background image, but rather "floats" in front of the background. Graphic Objects are discussed in detail later on in this chapter.

Adding Clip Art

The *Add Clip Art...* command in the **File** menu lets you select a *portion* of a graphic image from any graphic image source (see *Graphic Image Sources*, earlier in this chapter). The process involves three basic steps:

- Selecting a graphic image either from disk, video or QuickTake camera.

- Positioning the clip art on the card.

- Placing the clip art on the card, where it becomes a part of the card's background.

To add a piece of clip art:

1. Select **File** menu: *Add Clip Art...*

2. Use the standard file dialog to select a graphic image file; or, select the source of the graphic image if you have a video digitizer or QuickTake camera.

3. The image is displayed in a window titled **Clip Art**.

   - This clip art window allows you to select a portion of the graphic image to be used as clip art. To select a different graphic image file, click the *Get another picture...* button and the standard dialog will once again be displayed.

File	
New Stack	
Open Stack...	⌘O
Save Stack	⌘S
Save Stack As...	
Import Background...	⌘I
Export Screen...	⌘E
Add Clip Art...	⌘A
Page Setup...	
Print...	⌘P
Print to Video...	
Quit HyperStudio	⌘Q

▲▲▲

Add Clip Art... is located in the **File** menu.

▲▲▲
The Clip Art window

- Sometimes a graphic image is larger than will fit inside the Clip Art window. Use the scroll bars located on the right and bottom of the window to view more of the image.

4. In the clip art window, use the Rectangle Selector Tool or the Lasso to select a portion of the image you want to use as clip art.

   - These tools work the same as those found in the **Tools** menu. As a shortcut, you can double-click them to automatically select the entire graphic image.

   - Double-clicking either of the tools will also allow you to select an image that is larger than the clip art window.

5. Once you have selected the portion of the image you want, click on the **OK** button. Should you decide not to add clip art at this time, click on **Cancel**.

6. After you click **OK** in the Clip Art window, the selection will be centered on the card with the flashing dots surrounding it.

7. Position the clip art on the card by moving the cursor inside the flashing dots and *dragging* it to a new location.

8. While the clip art is still selected—the flashing dots are still active—you can:

   - Re-size or rotate the clip art using *Scale & Rotate* in the **Edit** menu.

   - If you used the Rectangle Selector Tool while in the Clip Art window, re-size the image by clicking and dragging on any corner of the flashing dots.

9. Click on the *outside* of the flashing dots to *place* the clip art onto the card where it becomes a part of the overall background image.

The Paint Tools

The paint tools are located on the lower section of the tool palette and are used for creating and editing a card's background image.

Certain paint tool operations can be modified with a key combination—holding down the Shift key while using the oval tool, for example, will produce perfect circles. Also, if you have "torn off" the tool palette from the menu bar, double-clicking many of the icons will display additional options. See **Appendix A-Quick Reference**, for a complete list of all the tools and their associated key combinations.

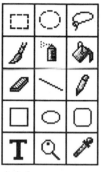

▲▲▲
The paint tools

Selection Tools

The selection tools—Rectangle Selector, Circle Selector and Lasso—are used for selecting portions of the background image. Once an area is selected with any of these tools, there are a number of options you can use to modify the selection. The following options are available from the **Edit** menu:

Cut (⌘-X):

This removes the selected area from the background image and places a copy of the selection on the clipboard where it can later be pasted on the current card, another card, or even another stack.

Copy (⌘-C):

This places a copy of the selection on the clipboard where it can later be pasted on the current card, another card, or even another stack.. Unlike cut, the image is not removed from the background.

Clear (Delete key):

This removes the selected area from the background image. It does not place a copy on the clipboard.

Reference

Deselecting Images

- To deselect an image, or to make a new selection, click *outside* the flashing dots, or simply select any other tool from the Tools menu.

Moving Selected Images

- To move a selected image to a new location on the card, click *inside* the flashing dots and *drag* the image to a new location.

Making A Quick Copy

- You can copy a selection by holding down the Option key and *dragging* it . This method has two advantages: 1) it's a quick way to copy an image; and, 2) the copy is not placed on the clipboard, thus keeping whatever image *is* on the clipboard unchanged.
- Shift-Option at the beginning of the drag will constrain the motion of the copy to be perfectly aligned, either vertically or horizontally, depending on the direction the mouse first moved.

TIP

Undo that painting!

- If you change your mind or make a mistake after painting on the card background, just choose "Undo" in the Edit menu (or type Command-Z). You can only undo your most recent painting action— for example, if you draw three lines with the Paint Brush tool, then select "Undo," only two lines will remain.

Paste (⌘-V)

When a copy of an image has been placed on the clipboard—by using either the Cut or Copy commands—using *Paste* will place a copy of the image onto the current card. It is placed in the same *screen position* that it was originally copied—even if you are pasting it to a different card or another stack. You can paste a copied image as many times as you like; it remains on the clipboard until you cut or copy something else.

Effects in the Edit menu provide these additional options:

Flip Sideways

Flips the selected area left to right, and vice-versa. *Not available with the Lasso.*

Flip Upside Down

Flips the selected area upside down, and vice-versa. *Not available with the Lasso.*

Scale & Rotate

Allows you to change the size of the selected image, and/or rotate the selection to a specified degree. *Rotation is not available with the Lasso.*

Replace Colors

Replaces or swaps two different colors within the selected area.

Gradients

Paints a graduated transition of two different colors within the selected area.

Rectangle Selector Tool

⬚ This tool allows you to select a rectangular area. When this tool is active, the cursor changes to a crosshair.

To make a selection, position the cursor at one corner of the desired area, click and

TIP

Shortcuts for the Selector tool

- Double-click the Selector tool icon to select the entire background.

- Grab a corner of the selected area, and drag the mouse to stretch or shrink the selected area.

- Press Shift-Control-Tab to switch between the Selector and Browse tools.

- Hold down the Option key while dragging the mouse to create a copy without moving the original. • Press the delete key to delete a selected area.

Shortcuts for the Circle Selector tool

- Hold down the Option key while dragging the mouse to create a copy without moving the original.

- Press the delete key to delete a selected area.

Tricks for the Lasso tool

- Double-click the Lasso tool icon to Lasso the entire background.

- Hold down the Command key while selecting an area to do a "pencil Lasso".

- Hold down the Option key while clicking inside an area to do an "expanding Lasso" selection.

- Hold down the Option key while dragging a selected area to make a copy without moving the original.

- It is not necessary to select an entire area with the Lasso. The Lasso will "close the loop", drawing a straight line to where your selection started.

- To copy another area's pattern or color, select an area with the Lasso. Choose "Copy" from the Edit menu while pressing the Option key. This is a good way to copy an unusual area or pattern.

drag the mouse to enclose the selection. Then release the mouse button. A blinking dotted line will indicate the selected area.

If you cut, delete or move a selected area, it will be replaced by a solid color. The color used is determined by the color located at the point in which you first clicked the mouse to start your selection.

Circle Selector Tool

⊡ This tool is similar to the Square Selector Tool, except that it allows you to select a circular area. When this tool is active, the cursor changes to a crosshair.

To make a selection, position the cursor at one corner of the desired area, press the mouse button and drag the mouse while holding the mouse button down. After you release the mouse button, flashing dots will indicate the selected area.

If you cut, delete or move a selected area, it will be replaced by a solid color. The color used is determined by the color located at the point in which you first clicked the mouse to start your selection.

Lasso tool

⊘ Use this tool to select an image on a solid-colored background by drawing a freehand line around the object to be selected. When you release the mouse button, the color at the point you started the Lasso determines the background color. Only the parts of the image different from that background are selected with an outline.

Painting Tools

The painting tools—Paint Brush, Spray Paint and Paint Bucket—use the currently selected color or pattern to paint images on the background. To select the color or pattern for painting with any of these tools, click on the Color palette (if it is "torn" off

TIP

Tricks for the Paintbrush

- Double-click the Paint Brush tool to go directly to the "Brush Shape..." dialog.
- Hold down the shift key to paint only straight lines.

Tricks for the Spray Paint tool

- Use the Colors menu to select a new color or pattern.
- Carefully using the spray tool with slightly lighter or darker color than a shape on the screen can create effective highlights and shadows. See the "Art Lesson" stack on the CD in the "Advanced Techniques" section!

the menu bar) or select from the **Colors** menu. *For more information on the color palette, see* Working With Color *later in this chapter.*

Paint Brush

The Paint Brush uses the current brush shape to allow you to draw freehand in the current color or pattern. Select *Brush Shape...* from the **Options** menu to pick a new brush shape, or double-click on the Paint Brush icon on the **Tools** menu.

Spray Paint Tool

This tool paints a scattered pattern of dots in the current color or pattern. You can click repeatedly over an area while moving the mouse very slightly for a "repeat spray" effect, or drag it for a "scattered" effect. While using the Spray Paint Tool, move the mouse quickly for a more diffused pattern, or slowly for a denser pattern.

Paint Bucket

The Paint Bucket, also known as the **Fill Tool**, (shown as a tipped paint can with paint pouring out) is used to fill an enclosed area with a solid color or pattern. The tip of the cursor (the very end of the paint pouring out of the can) is where the fill originates. Be sure that the area you wish to fill is completely enclosed; gaps will cause "leakage." If the fill covers a larger area than you intended, choose "Undo" from the Edit menu, then check the boundaries of your area. (Use the Magnifying Glass tool to help find small gaps.)

Eraser Tool

The Eraser tool is a handy way to erase an area of the screen. (It's the similar to drawing with a rectangular brush using the background color.) To use it, press and hold the mouse button while dragging over the area you want to erase.

Tricks for the Eraser tool

- Double-click the eraser when the tools menu is torn off to erase the entire screen to the background color. (If you do this by accident, immediately select "Undo" from the Edit menu.)

- Hold down the Shift key while dragging the mouse to erase in a straight line.

Tricks for the Line tool

- Select "Line Size..." from the Options menu, or double-click the Line tool icon, to choose a new line size.

- Select "Draw Multiple" from the Options menu to leave lines on the screen as you drag the mouse.

- Select "Draw Centered" from the Options menu to draw from a centered point instead of the end.

- Use the Colors menu to select a new color or pattern.

- Hold down the Shift key to draw only straight lines.

Tricks for the Pencil

- Double-click the Pencil tool icon to enter the magnifier mode.

- Hold down the Command key while you click on a color on the screen to change the current paint color.

- Hold down the Shift key to draw only straight lines.

Tricks for the Rectangle tool

- Select "Draw Filled" from the Options menu to draw a solid rectangle.

- Select "Draw Center" from the Options menu to draw from a center point instead of a corner.

- Select "Line Size" from the Options menu to change the size of the rectangle's outline.

- Hold down the Shift key to draw perfect squares.

There are several ways to set the color that the eraser uses

1. Use *Set Eraser Color...* in the **Options** menu. A dialog appears allowing you to select a color. Clicking the **Erase Screen** button in this dialog, will cause the entire screen to be immediately erased to the specified background color.

2. Selecting a color from the Colors menu while holding down the Option key.

3. Use the Eye Dropper with the Option key down and click on the background.

Drawing Tools

The drawing tools—Line Tool, Pencil, Rectangle Tool, Oval Tool and Rounded Rectangle Tool— are used for drawing shapes on the background. Each tool uses the currently selected color or pattern for drawing images.

Line Tool

This is used to draw straight lines in the current color or pattern. Press the mouse button where you want the line to begin. Drag the mouse. Notice that while the mouse button is down, you can move the end of the line anywhere. Release the button where you want the line to end.

Pencil

With the Pencil tool, you can draw freehand shapes in the currently selected color or pattern. The Pencil tool is also available in the *magnification* mode (See Magnifier Tool, later in this chapter).

Rectangle Tool

This tool easily allows you to draw a rectangle.

To use the Rectangle Tool, press the mouse button and hold it down while you drag the rectangle to size. Release the button when the rectangle is the desired size.

Rounded Rectangle Tool

☐ This tool draws allows you to draw a rectangle with rounded corners.

To use the Rounded Rectangle Tool, press the mouse button and hold it down while you drag the rectangle to size. Release the button when the rectangle is the desired size.

Oval tool

○ This is similar to the rectangle tools, except it draws an oval shape. The point where you press the mouse button represents the upper-left corner of an imaginary rectangle. It contains the oval being drawn. The point where you release the mouse button represents the lower-right corner.

Other Paint Tools

Text Tool

T This tool is used to paint text onto the background. This is not the same as adding a Text Object: a Text Object is an independent object that can be moved and edited at any time; the Text Tool, on the other hand, paints the text, where it becomes a part of the overall background image. To use the Text Tool:

1. Select the Text Tool from the **Tools** menu; the pointer changes to the text cursor.

2. Place the text cursor where you want to start typing. Click the mouse once.

3. The text cursor will disappear and a blinking cursor will appear on the background. This is where the text will begin.

TIP

Tricks for the Oval tool
- Select "Draw Filled" from the Options menu to draw a solid oval. (When this item isn't marked, you only draw the outline of an oval. Note that you may double-click the icon to toggle the "draw Filled" option on and off.
- Select "Draw Multiple" from the Options menu to leave multiple ovals on the screen as you drag the mouse.
- Select "Draw Centered" from the Options menu to draw from a center point instead of a corner.
- Select "Line Size" from the Options menu to change the size of the oval's outline.
- Hold down the Shift key to draw circles instead of ovals.

Tricks for the Text tool
- To change the size, color, and font, select "Text Style" from the Options menu. You can also double-click on the Text tool's icon.
- Use the Colors menu to select a new color or pattern.

4. Begin typing.

You can change the type style at any time, even while typing. However, once you reposition the text cursor (by clicking the mouse in a new location on the screen) or choose another paint tool, the text becomes part of the background image. See also *Chapter 6, Text*.

Magnifying Glass

🔍 This is a special mode for magnifying the background image. You can edit the screen dots on a pixel level with the paint tools—allowing you to make very small changes to the background image. (This is sometimes called the "zoom" mode.)

1. When you select this tool, the cursor will change to a magnifying glass.

2. Click the center of the cursor over the area you want to examine. You will see a magnified image of the area of the screen in the rectangle, with a normal view of the same area in the upper-left corner of the screen. Click again to get a higher magnification level.

3. To return to normal view, select **Options**: *Magnify—100%*; or click the mouse in the small regular sized image; or press the Escape key.

Eye Dropper

✐ The Eye Dropper tool is used to "pick up" a color of the background so that you can use that color with the other paint tools. If a particular color is difficult to match or find in the color palette, the Eye Dropper tool will assist you in finding the exact color you may need—even if it doesn't appear in the color palette.

1. Click on the color you wish to "pick up" with the Eye Dropper tool.

2. That color will appear in the window at the bottom of the color palette.

TIP

Special Tricks With the Magnifying Glass

- Holding down the Option key will change the cursor to a hand, which allows you to scroll the screen by simply dragging in any direction.

- Clicking in the regular sized image (in the upper-left corner of the screen) will take you out of this magnifying mode. You can also get back to 100% magnification by pressing the Escape key or Command period.

- Select a new color to paint with from the Colors menu, or hold down the Command key and click a pixel to select its color.

- Attempting to paint a pixel that is already in the current color will flip the Pencil tool over and use the eraser end: the Pencil will then "erase" in the background color. Releasing the mouse button immediately changes the Pencil tool back to normal.

Graphic Objects

Graphic Objects are similar to clip art in that they are "small pieces of art"—yet they differ in that they do not modify the background image. Rather, Graphic Objects "float" in front of the background image and retain their own identity as individual objects. They can be moved, re-sized, deleted, and even have *actions* assigned to them—just as with other objects, such as Buttons, for example.

Adding A Graphic Object

The *Add a Graphic Object...* command from the **Objects** menu, lets you select a portion of a graphic image from any graphic image source (see *Graphic Image Sources*, earlier in this chapter) for use as a Graphic Object. Adding a Graphic Object involves five basic steps:

- Selecting a graphic image either from disk, video or QuickTake camera;
- Positioning the Graphic Object on the card;
- Placing the Graphic Object; by clicking on the outside of the flashing dots;
- Determining the "appearance" of the Graphic Object;
- And, as an option, assigning actions to the Graphic Object.

To add a Graphic Object:

1. Select **Objects**: *Add a Graphic Object...*
2. Use the standard file dialog to select a graphic image file; or, select the source of the graphic image if you have a video digitizer or QuickTake camera.
3. The image is displayed in a window titled **Graphic Objects**.
   - This window allows you to select a portion of the graphic image. To select a different graphic image file, click the *Get another picture...* button and the standard dialog will once again be displayed.

- Sometimes a graphic image is larger than will fit inside the Graphic Objects window. Use the scroll bars located on the right and bottom of the window to view more of the image.

4. In the Graphic Objects window, use the Rectangle Selector Tool or the Lasso to select a portion of the image you want to use as clip art.

   - These tools work the same as those found in the **Tools** menu. As a shortcut, you can double-click them to automatically select the entire graphic image.

5. Once you have selected the portion of the image you want, click on the **OK** button. Should you decide not to add a Graphic Object, click on **Cancel**.

6. After you click **OK** in the Graphic Objects window, the selection will be centered on the card with the flashing dots surrounding it.

7. Position the Graphic Object on the card by moving the cursor inside the flashing dots and *dragging* it to a new location..

8. Click on the *outside* of the flashing dots to *place* the object onto the card.

9. The Graphic Appearance dialog appears.

The Graphic Appearance dialog
▼▼▼

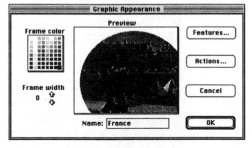

Graphic Object Appearance

At this point, HyperStudio will display the *Graphic Appearance* dialog, where you can set certain attributes of the Graphic Object:

Frame Width

To adjust the frame's width, click the up or down arrows. If you don't want a frame with your graphic, click the down arrow until the frame disappears.

Features

Clicking the "Features..." button will bring up the Item Features dialog box. This dialog box is divided into two halves.

Graphic Object info

The upper portion tells you the type of graphic object, the amount of memory it occupies, the "owner" card (where the objects definition is stored), the graphic object's ID, and the object's position on the card. The object's ID and position can be useful for certain HyperLogo commands, which require either an object's ID number or name.

Actions

When creating a Graphic Object, many Actions can be assigned to the graphic such as play a sound, go to the next card, play a movie, etc. by clicking on the Actions button in the Graphic Appearance window. Next, choose the actions you wish your graphic to perform from the Actions window that appears. Complete defining your Graphic Object and when you click on the Graphic Object on your card it will trigger the specified actions.

Graphic Object Features

Locked

With this box checked, the graphic object can not be moved or edited.

Group Item

Any object with this item checked will show up on all cards within the same group. If you unmark this check box, the button will no longer be a group item and will appear only on the card you were at when you unchecked this box. Marking the box will cause the object to once again be shared with all of the cards in the group.

Hidden

When the Hidden check box is marked, the entire graphic object is invisible. (It will show up, however, when you switch to the Edit tool or Graphic tool.)

Draggable

If this option is marked, the user can drag the graphic around the screen with the Browse tool. This can be useful for Drop off buttons, which are triggered when a graphic is dropped onto them.

Cursor

You can choose a special cursor that will be associated with your Graphic Object by clicking and holding the mouse button on the button labeled "None".

Deleting a Graphic Object

Select the Graphic Object edit tool found in the top section of the Tool Box labeled with a "G" (This is one of the specialized editing tools). The Graphic Object edit tool will let you edit all the graphic objects on the current card. Use it by clicking once on a graphic object to select it, and then you can re-size it, move it, or cut, copy, or delete it (Press the "delete" Key on your keyboard).

Re-sizing a Graphic Object

Select the Graphic Object edit tool found in the top section of the Tool Box labeled with a "G" (This is one of the specialized editing tools). The Graphic Object edit tool will let you edit all the graphic objects on the current card. Use it by clicking once on a graphic object to select it, and then you can re-size it by moving your cursor to an edge or corner of the object. The cursor will turn into a double-headed arrow. Drag the edge or corner of the Graphic Object to re-size it.

HideShow NBA

This NBA allows you to hide or show a Graphic Object, a Button, or a Text Object. You can achieve impressive "special effects" by pre-hiding graphic objects, then showing them at the click of a button. Possibilities include fake dialog boxes, "pop-up

▲▲▲
Hide Show NBA dialog.

menus" and more.

To use the HideShow NBA, simply select it from the NBA menu and then click "Use this NBA". You will be prompted for three things:

Specify the name of the object you wish to work with, (If you have only one Text Object, Graphic Object or Button on the card, you do not have to enter the object name to be shown, hidden or flipped.)

Select the type of object (Graphic Object, Text Object, or Button), and whether you want to hide it, show it, or flip it (that is hide it if it's visible, or show it if it's already hidden.)

SlideShow NBA

With the click of a button you can display all of the pictures in a specified folder. Once you've clicked on "Use this NBA" in the New Button Actions dialog box, you will be prompted to select a folder. Click on "Open" to find a folder within a folder. Click on "Select" to choose the folder that holds the pictures you wish to display.

There are a number of options:

Continuously display files: If you mark this option the slide show will run continuously. When it reaches the last picture in the directory, the slide show will start again.

Leave last picture on exit: By marking this option, when the slide show finishes, the last screen displayed will remain on the card.

Show filename on pictures: This will display the filename on the lower-right corner of the screen.

Time delay: The "Time Delay" window lets you specify how quickly the slide show runs. Smaller numbers make the slide show faster.

Folder to Show: The folder which you have selected will appear. Click on OK to confirm your choices.

The SlideShow NBA options dialog.
▼▼▼

HyperStudio SlideShow NBA
Select options:
☐ Continuously display files
☐ Leave last picture on exit
☐ Show filename on picture(s)

Time delay (0-9): 2 seconds

Folder to show   Cancel   OK

HS Art

▲▲▲
3-dimensional boxes are made easy with the BoxMaker!

BoxMaker Extra

BoxMaker can be found under the Extras menu. BoxMaker allows you to create 3D boxes in two easy steps:

1. Draw a rectangle, after choosing BoxMaker, to make the front or the back of the box.

2. Move the remaining part of the box to the desired location and click. The box may be made to appear solid by using the Fill tool with colors or patterns to fill in the sides.

Chapter 6
Text

HyperStudio provides two methods for displaying text on a card: **Text Objects** and the **Text tool**. A Text Object is an independent object that can be moved and edited at any time, while the Text tool paints the text on the screen which becomes a permenant part of the background. Although each method of displaying text is different, they both have two common features: *style and quality*.

Text Style

The way text looks on the screen is called the "style" of the text, or better yet, the "text style." To determine the text style, HyperStudio provides the **Text Style dialog** (see illustration on this page). This dialog allows you to pre-determine how your text will appear before you begin typing. You can also use the Text Style dialog to change the style after it has already been typed (however, there are limitations for painted text, which you will see later on). Text styles consist of several different features:

1. **Font**: such as Times, Helvetica, Chicago;
2. **Color**: red blue, green, etc.;
3. **Size**: measured in *points*; and,
4. **Attributes**: such as bold, italic, underlined, and so on.

Notice also that a sample of the text, as you have selected it, will appear in the upper-right corner of the dialog box. This makes it easy to see how your text will appear before you click "OK"!

Text Quality

How well your text appears on the screen, or its *visual quality*, depends on the background color and the basic design of the font you're using. In general, contrasting background and foreground colors, large type sizes, and legible fonts will all contribute to a clear, easy-to-read display.

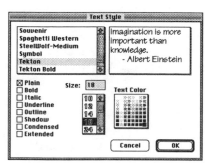

▲▲▲
The Text Style dialog: To use this dialog, select Text Style from the Options menu, or use the keyboard shortcut: command-Y.

Painting Text

To paint text onto the background, select the Text tool from the Tools palette.

▼▼▼

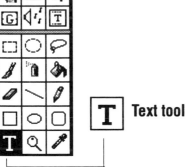

 Text tool

Introduction to the Text Tool

Like all the other paint tools—the square tool, line tool, circle tool, etc.—the Text tool actually **paints** directly onto the background of the card. The difference, of course, is that the Text tool paints with characters of the alphabet that can form words, sentences, and paragraphcs.

Using The Text Tool

When you choose the Text tool from the **Tools** menu, the pointer changes to the text placement cursor. To paint text onto the background, place the cursor where you want to start typing and click the mouse once. The text cursor dissappears and is replaced by a blinking vertical line. Now simply begin typing and the text will appear on the screen!

As mentioned before, the way your text appears on the screen depends on the current "text style" of the text you're typing. If you decide to change the style after you have already begun typing, select *Text Style…* from the **Options** menu to get the Text Style dialog. Changes made in the Text Style dialog will then appear when you click "OK".

Note: If you want to change the style of the text after you have begun typing, you must do so *before* you click anywhere else on the screen or select a different tool. Doing either of these will "set" the text to the background. Thus, any changes in the text style will not effect text that has already been painted.

Editing Painted Text

If you make a mistake while typing, you can use the Delete Key for backing up and deleting the most recently typed characters. Use the Clear Key to delete all text that has been recently typed. Once text has been painted and set to the background, it can be moved, erased, or otherwise edited the same as any other image that is a part of the card's background.

Special Text Tool Effects

There are many ways to create eye-catching titles on your cards with the Text tool. Below are examples of some of the more popular techniques you can use:

Progressive Disclosure:

Give your audience a little information at a time by clicking on consecutive cards to slowly reveal your entire message. For example, create 4 cards with the same 4 lines of text on each. Starting with the third card, erase one line of your text. Move to the second card and erase two lines of text. Move to the first card and erase 3 lines of the text. Then, place large invisible buttons over cards one, two and three. Program each button to go to the next card with *Fastest*, *Left to Right* or *Right to Left* as the transition. When you click on the cards from one to three, your message will appear one line at a time until the entire message is on screen.

Cookie Cutter Effect:

Imagine a boldly written word. Now imagine picking up a pattern from a picture so that the letters are written in that pattern. To do this, we create a card with a pattern on it. Then we create a second card, which will become our "working" card where we will write our text. What we'll do is lasso the text and bring it over to the pattern. We'll then pick up the pattern from the first card and bring our new text back. You will have the choice of having the text cut out the patter (just like a cookie cutter), or not disturbing the original pattern (imagine a cookie copier). This effect works on shapes too!

A Progressive Disclosure Sample:

Card 1

> *Welcome to...*

Card 2

> *Welecome to...*
> *Great Ideas*

Card 3

> *Welcome to...*
> *Great Idea*
> *and Tricks*

Card 4

> *Welcome to...*
> *Great Idea*
> *and Tricks*
> *with HyperStudio!*

Text Objects

Text Objects provide a method for displaying text on the screen that, unlike painted text, can be easily edited. A Text Object is defined within a rectangular area on the card. Within this rectangle you can type text, edit text, and even "scroll" the text if there are more words than can fit within the defined area. In addition to typing, you can also import text created in other wordprocessor programs such as TeachText, ClarisWorks™ or MS Word™, to name a few.

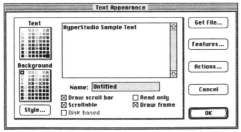

Adding a Text Object

The Text Appearance dialog
▼▼▼

Adding A Text Object

Follow these steps to add a Text Object to a card:

1. Select ***Add a Text Object...*** (Cmd—T) from the **Objects** menu.

2. A rectangle appears on the screen. Use this rectangle to determine both the size and postion of the Text Object. *Drag from the center of the rectangle to position it on the card; drag from the corners or sides to change the rectangle's size.*

3. When you have the Text Object's rectangle positioned as you like it, click *outside* of the rectangle—or press the Return Key—to "set" it in place. You will then be presented with the Text Appearance dialog showing an example of your Text Object, its attributes, and the item's name. After setting the Text Appearance options, click "OK".

Text Appearance and Attributes

The Text Appearance dialog allows you to define certain features to the Text Object. Following is a description of each of these options:

☒ **Draw scroll bar**: Draws a scroll bar on the right side of the Text Object, allowing the user to move vertically through the contents of the Text Object.

☒ **Allow scrolling**: Allows the user to scroll through the Text Object with the arrow keys or a scroll bar (assuming "Draw scroll bar" is marked, above).

⊠ **Read only**: With this check box on, text cannot be typed, thus preventing the user from changing the text in your Text Object. If you don't want people typing in your Text Object, or wish to make the cursor disappear, choose this option after you've finished typing your text. To access the Text Info box at a later time, use the Text edit tool or the universal edit tool (the pointer) to select the Text Object. Then choose *Edit this Text Object...* from the **Objects** menu. (Note that disk-based text is always read-only, and will have the *Read only* check box dimmed.)

⊠ **Draw Frame**: If this option is marked, HyperStudio will draw a thin frame around the boundary of your Text Object.

⊠ **Get File**: To use a file from disk, click the "Get File..." button. You'll see the standard file dialog, which allows you to choose a standard text file. (Keep in mind that each Text Object is limited to 32K.) The file will be loaded and the text will appear in the Text Object.

As an experienced user you can select a file from disk. After you have clicked on Get File, the disk-based option will become active. If you choose disk-based text, HyperStudio uses the most updated version of the text file each time you open the stack.

You can get text from the **Internet** using options built into HyperStudio. MediaLink files (see MediaLink documentation in the Internet section) may be accessed through the Get File button when creating a Text Object. You'll see the standard file dialog, which allows you to choose a MediaLink file as well as other files on the disk. Provided that you have an open connection to the Internet, the MediaLink file will locate specified text from the Internet and that text will appear in your Text Object!

⚪ **Style...:** By selecting the style button, you are brought to the Text Style dialog box. (See also the Text Style section, earlier in this chapter).

TIP

What are those three little dots...

- You may have noticed that some menu items, and certain options in dialogs, have three little dots after their names. This simply means that the particular option requires some additional input from you—usually via another dialog.

- When you click inside a Text Object, select a passage of text, or use the Pointer or Text Edit tool to select an entire Text Object, selecting Text Style... from the Options menu is a useful way to quickly see what style was used in that particular Text Object.

The Text Style dialog
▼▼▼

Editing a Text Object

Text Objects can be edited, even after they have been created. The following techniques explain how to edit and change features of a Text Object:

Changing the Style of a Text Object

To change the style of a Text Object, first select the object with the Text Edit or Pointer tools, then choose Text Style... from the Options menu. Notice that this method also allows you to specify the background color in addition to the foreground (text) color. Although individual letters and words of a Text Object may have different colors, only one background color can be used for the entire Text Object. You can also align the text within a Text Object—left, right, or center justified—but keep in mind that all text within the object is affected.

Resizing a Text Object:

You can resize and reposition a Text Object with the Text Edit or Pointer tools. Click once on the Text Object to select it, then drag the corners of the enclosing rectangle to change its size. To move the object, click in the center and drag it to its new location

Changing a Text Object's Attributes

To edit a Text Object's attributes, simply double-click on it. You can also select it with the Text Edit or Pointer tools and choose *Edit this Text Object...* from the **Edit** menu. The Text Appearance dialog will be displayed where you can change the object's attributes.

Deleting a Text Object

Selecting the Text Edit or Pointer tool from the Tools menu displays all the Text Objects on the current card, even the "invisible" ones.. To delete a Text Object, first select it by clicking once on it and then delete it by pressing the Delete Key on the keyboard. You can also use Clear Text Object from the Edit menu to delete a selected Text Object.

Editing Text Within a Text Object

In addition to being able to edit Text Objects, you can also edit the individual text within the object. The following techniques describe how to do this:

Changing the Style within a Text Object

To change the style of individual selections of text, make sure the Text Object is not a *Read Only* item. Select the text you want to change by dragging your cursor over it to highlight the word or phrase. You can change the selected text color by simply selecting a color from the color palette. To change the style of the selected text, use *Text Style...* from the **Options** menu.

Cutting, Copying and Clearing Text

To copy or cut a portion of the text within a Text Object, select a passage of text and then choose either *Copy Text* or *Cut Text* from the **Edit** menu. When using *Copy Text* a copy of the selected text is placed onto the internal "clipboard" where it can later be pasted into another Text Object, or elsewhere within the same object. Using *Cut Text* also places the selected text onto the clipboard, however the text is removed from the Text Object. Selecting *Clear Text* will remove the text without copying it to the clipboard.

Pasting Text

Text that has been copied or cut (see the previous paragraph) can be pasted into any Text Object in the current stack, or other stacks. To do this, click the text cursor just after the position where you want the pasted text to appear. Then select Past text from the Edit menu, or use Cmd-V. The text that is currently on the clipboard will be pasted into the Text Object.

Exporting Text to Disk

Text within a Text Object can be saved to disk as a "text" file (also known as an

TIP

Copying and Pasting Text Styles

What if you wanted to assign a set of style settings from one text field to another? That is, if you wanted to copy-and-paste the text font, styles—such as bold, italic, etc.—and the color, but not the text itself. Here's how you do it:

• Select the first text field, and choose "Text Style" from the Options menu (or just press Command—Y). When the style dialog appears, verify the styles visually, and then choose "Cancel." Now, the trick: select the second text field, but this time press Shift-Apple-Y (or hold down the shift key while you select "Text Style" from the Options menu). The old style will be carried into the style dialog. Clicking "OK" at this point will then set the second text field to the style of the first. This can be very useful if you have to change the style settings of several different text fields.

"ASCII" file). To do this, select the Text Object with the Text Edit or Pointer tools and then choose Export text from the File menu. You will be given the option to give the file a name with the standard Save dialog.

Text Object Features

⊠ **Group Text Object:** A Text Object with this item checked will show up on all cards within the same group. This means that the Text Object's location and attributes (color and style) will be repeated on all group cards, but the contents of the Text Object will be unique.

If you unmark the Group Text Object check box, the object will no longer be a group item and will appear only on the card you were at when you unchecked this box. Marking the box will cause the Text Object to once again be shared with all of the cards in the group.

There is one exception to the contents of a group Text Object not being shared across all cards: You can edit the text within grouped Text Objects on individual cards. In other words, changing the text in a group object on one card will not effect the text on any of the other Text Objects within that particular group.

⊠ **Transparent Text Object:** If "Transparent" is marked after clicking on the Features button, the background of the Text Object will be transparent-the text will "float over" whatever is underneath it. This can be a very nice effect, especially if you set the Text Object's attributes so that HyperStudio does not draw a frame around the object or a scroll bar. Note that if you try to edit or scroll the text, the Text Object will immediately become opaque.

⊠ **Locked Text Object:** With the "Locked" option box checked, the Text Object may not be moved or edited.

Item Features

Item Type: Text Field
Space Used: 166 bytes
Item Owner: 1
Item ID: 2
Item Card Position: 1

☐ Locked   ☐ Hidden
☐ Group item   ☐ Transparent

[✐ ▼]   [Cancel]   [OK]

▲▲▲
The Text Features dialog.
Available to experienced users only.

⊠ **Hidden Text Object:** When the Hidden check box is marked after clicking on the Features button, the entire Text Object is invisible. (It will show up, however, when you switch to the Edit tool or Text Object Edit tool.)

Printing a Text Object

In order to print the contents of a Text Object, you must first click in the Text Object, then choose Print from the File menu.

Find Text (Command-F)

With this command, you can search for a word or phrase in all of the Text Objects in the current stack. HyperStudio starts searching from the first Text Object on the current card.

You can search the editable or read-only items on each card, or both. Clicking the "Case sensitive" check box will limit the search to text that matches the letters exactly you typed, while clicking the "Wrap around search" check box tells HyperStudio to search the entire stack, not just from the current card to the end of the stack. Click "Find" (or press Return) to start the search. To continue searching for the same word or phrase again, press Shift-Command-F.

Hypertext Links

Hypertext is text that can be clicked on and in doing so cause some kind of action to occur. For example, you could click on a word in a Text Object and be taken to another card that shows a picture and text that more fully describes that single word. Or you could click on a phrase within a Text Object which plays a sound, activates an animation or perform any other action that a button could perform.. Hypertext can be very powerful and expand concepts you wish to convey.

```
┌─────────────────────────────────────┐
│            Find Text                 │
│  ╔═══════════════════════════════╗   │
│  Search for: [                 ]     │
│                                      │
│  Search in:                          │
│   ● All fields      □ Case sensitive │
│   ○ Editable fields ⊠ Wrap around search │
│   ○ Read-only fields                 │
│                                      │
│   ( Cancel )        (  Find  )       │
│  ╚═══════════════════════════════╝   │
└─────────────────────────────────────┘
```

▲▲▲
The Find Text dialog

TIP

• The Find Text... command only works on Text Objects. It cannot "see" words painted by the text painting tool from the Tools menu.

• When using "Find Text…" in a locked stack with a password set (in the Preferences dialog box), text cannot be found beyond the current card.

Use **Hypertext** to assign actions to a word or phrase.
▼▼▼

Hypertext is created by setting up "links" with selected text and actions. To create hypertext, first make a Text Object by choosing Add a Text Object under the Objects menu. Click in the Text Object, type some text into your Text Object and select the text you wish to become hypertext by dragging your cursor over it. Next, go to the Objects menu and choose Hypertext Links. Click Add link then, click on the "Action" button and choose the action or actions you wish to trigger. Click Done. Now, when you click on the hypertext word or phrase in your Text Object the action you programmed will be performed.

Roll Credits NBA

You can automatically scroll a text field at any rate. This can lend itself to interesting effects and is also very good for a "rolling credits" display, similar to the credits at the end of a movie.

To use the **Roll Credits NBA**, simply select it from the NBA menu and then click "Use this NBA".

First, you need to specify: the name of the Text Object, only if you have more than one Text Object on the same card as the button. You can actually leave all the default settings and just click on OK if you only have one Text Object on the card!

You can control how smooth the scroll is by choosing one of the following options:

Scroll lines

Marking this option will cause the text field to scroll a line at a time.

Scroll pixels

Marking this option will cause the field to scroll on a pixel-by-pixel level instead of line-by-line. If you mark this option, you should specify how many pixels (per scroll) you want the display to move. Enter this number at "# of pixels".

To make the credits scroll completely on to and off the screen, start and end the con-

▲▲▲
The Roll Credits NBA dialog

tents of the Text Object with several carriage returns-this will make a blank area that will be scrolled off at the beginning (with the credits coming in from the bottom), and then a blank area at the end of the credits which will be scrolled up (with the credits going off the top.)

Hide Show NBA

This NBA allows you to hide or show a Graphic Object, a Button, or a Text Object. You can achieve impressive "special effects" by pre-hiding graphic objects, then showing them at the click of a button. Possibilities include fake dialog boxes, "pop-up menus" and more.

To use the HideShow NBA, simply select it from the NBA menu and then click "Use this NBA". You will be prompted for three things:

Specify the name of the object you wish to work with, (If you have only one Text Object, Graphic Object or Button on the card, you do not have to enter the object name to be shown, hidden or flipped.)

Select the type of object (Graphic Object, Text Object, or Button) and whether you want to hide it, show it, or flip it (that is hide it if it's visible, or show it if it's already hidden.)

Ghostwriter

Enter text in the window and Ghostwriter will type it into the currently active Text Object on the card. If you want to designate a Text Object to be written in, then just write the name of the Text Object within curly brackets. You can also control the speed by typing fast or slow within curly brackets. The text will appear magically in the currently active Text Object on the card at the fastest speed.

Blabber Mouth

Using this NBA, your computer will read the text in a Text Object if you have Speech

▲▲▲
The HideShow NBA dialog

Manager installed on your Mac! You can also type in the name of a Text Object, and the text within that particular text container will be read. This works very well on the "A/V" Macintoshes as well!

Special Text Object Effects

Shadowed Text:

Create shadowed text by using two transparent Text Objects. Create a Text Object which has your title written in red. (Make the Text Object, type the title. Using the editing tool double-click on the Text Object, then make the Text Object Read only, not having a scroll bar or a frame. Make it transparent. Copy the Text Object by pressing Command -C.. Immediately press Command -V to paste the copy of the Text Object on that card. Double-click on the Text Object so you can change the color of the text. Make it black. Using the arrow keys move the Text Object two pixels to the left and two pixels up. Select the Browse tool to see the final effect. This is especially nice over a non-solid background.

Shadowed text using Text Objects

Chapter 7
Sound

You can have a sound play when a button is pressed. Choosing *Play a sound...* in the Actions dialog displays the Tape Deck dialog box. This will allow you to select an existing sound or record a new one. To play a sound, choose a sample sound and click the Play button to hear the sound. Click Disk Library to choose existing sounds from a disk file. HyperStudio comes with a collection of various sounds for you to use in your stacks. Click "Play" to verify the sound you want to add to your button, and that the volume is at an acceptable level. To use the sound, click "OK".

Recording Your Own Sounds

To record your own sound, choose *Play a sound...* in the **Actions** window when making the button or assigning an action to other objects. You will see the Tape deck dialog box. If you wish to record a new sound, and you have a microphone, click "Record." (Record is disabled if you don't have a microphone.) Watch the green level indicator as you record and verify that it is moving. If the indicator barely moves, then the sound is too soft. On the other hand, if the indicator is red, or is constantly at the top of its range, you're "over-driving" the microphone and the quality of your recording will suffer. Speak softer, and/or move the miccrophone further from your mouth.

The **Tape Deck** allows you to select sounds from the listed samples, from a sound file on disk, or record your own sound with a microphone.

▼▼▼

Watch the gas gauge—which appears only when recording—to see how much available memory you have used and how much memory remains. Digitized sound takes up about 5K for 10 seconds. Press any key or click the mouse to stop recording.

Click "Play" to hear your sound, and if you are not satisfied with the recording, simply record it again. When you are done, type a name for the new sound in the edit line (below the picture of the cassette tape) and click "OK". The sound will automatically be saved in the stack.

Stopping Sounds

At times, you may have sounds on previously visited cards that continue to play out

- The limit on the length of time for recording new sounds is determined by how much free memory is available when you record. If you have a large stack in memory, your "recordable" sounds will be shorter than when a stack is first started. So here's a tip for recording long sounds: if you're running out of space too quickly on your current stack, split the stack into segments to allow more "overhead" for recording or playing sounds. See the section on "memory" for additional information.

- Choosing "the stack" to store sounds can add to the overall size of your stack—possibly requiring more memory to run. You can use "in a separate file" to store your sounds on disk, thus reducing the amount of memory (RAM) needed to open and run your stack.

- Whether you use the "stack" method or the "separate file" method is entirely up to you. They both have their own advantages!

even though you may have moved to another card. To stop sounds from playing out when moving to another card, create an invisible Button on the new card or choose About this Card from the Objects menu and check "arriving at this card..." . Choose Play a sound... from the Actions window. When you see the Tape deck, choose "Stop all sounds" from the Sample sounds window and click OK. Click Automatic timer... in the Actions window, if you have created an invisible Button, and choose "Activate button as soon as card is shown". Click OK and Done.

When you move to a previous card with a sound and then move to the card with the "Stop all sounds" button or action, the sound from the previous card will not play out and will be stopped. This will not work, however, if the card with the sound playing has had "Background sound" checked in the Tape deck.

Disk-based Sounds

When in the Tape Deck, choosing "the stack" in the "Sound is stored in:" access box embeds your sound in the stack. This is useful if you want many buttons to share one sound.

Choosing "a separate file" in the "Sound is stored in:" access box will store your sound as a separate sound file. This is useful if you want many stacks to share the same sound file. It can be especially helpful if you record a live sound and want to easily have it available as a sound file for other uses.

Sounds from Internet:

This feature works with the Internet options built into HyperStudio. MediaLink files (please see MediaLink documentation in the Internet section of this reference) may be accessed by adding a button with sound. When choosing an existing sound by clicking "Disk Library..." in the Tape deck, you'll see the standard file dialog, which allows you to choose a MediaLink file as well as other files on the disk. Provided that you

TIP

Sound Quality

- When recording your own sound in the Tape deck, hold down the Command Key when you click "record" for better sound quality (although this mode uses twice as much memory for your recording).
- Speak firmly and clearly into the mike; try to use a "radio voice"! On some Apple-brand microphones, turning them to face away from you may actually improve the sound quality! (screen shot of Tape deck and "Stop all sounds" Sample here)

have an open connection to the Internet, the MediaLink file will locate a specified sound file from the Internet and that sound will appear in the Tape deck to be played and added to the button!

Sounds As QuickTime Movies

Most people have seen silent movies—pictures without sounds—but did you know QuickTime can do the opposite: play sounds without pictures? It's true! And this approach can be used to create very long sounds, or play sounds that would otherwise not be available in your stacks!

QuickTime movies can play MIDI sound files without the video. These sound files are very small in comparison to other files and so will allow you to use sound and music in your HyperStudio stack without taking up lots of disk space!

Before you begin, make sure you have the QuickTime 2.0, Apple Multimedia Tuner and QuickTime Musical Instruments extensions in your System folder. You will also need a QuickTime player application such as Simple Player.

1. Save a file using a MIDI Sequencing program like Musicshop as a MIDI file or download MIDI files from an online service or the Internet.

2. Start up the Simple Player program and "Open" the MIDI file from the File menu.

3. In Simple Player, go to the File menu and Save As. (This will allow you to save the MIDI file as a QuickTime Moov file.)

4. Click the "Options" button before Saving to make choices about how the MIDI file will sound when played.

5. Use your new QuickTime movie in HyperStudio by adding a button from the Objects menu and choosing "Play a Movie or Video" in the Actions window. In the Video/Movie Source window click "Disk file (QuickTime movies)". A standard file dialog box will appear and you can select your MIDI movie. Finish

programming your button and when you click on the button it will call up your MIDI movie. You will hear your MIDI sound file only, as the movie plays.

Mod Files & Other Sound Files Supported

HyperStudio supports AIFF sound format, System 7 sounds (sound resource files), HyperStudio Apple IIGS sounds, WAV sound files (PC files) and Mod sounds (music files). In addition, MIDI sound files may be played as a QuickTime movie soundtrack on a card (please see Sounds As QuickTime Movies). All of these types of sound files may be downloaded from the Internet.

Background Sounds

Marking the "Background sound" box when in the Tape deck will allow your sound file to play until it is finished, even if another sound button or a button going to another stack is clicked. (both of these actions will normally stop a sound before it is finished playing.)

Playing Sound From A CD-ROM

CD-ROM can consist of two distinct portions: Data, in the form of clip art, QuickTime movies, text, and digitized sounds. HyperStudio can access all of these items through the standard menu choices of Add clip art, Play a movie, etc. The second portion of some CD's are the audio tracks. To play these, you use the CD Play NBA.

The CD Play NBA dialog.
▼▼▼

To use this NBA, you will need version 4.02 or higher of the Apple CD-ROM Extension, or the appropriate CD-ROM driver available from the manufacturer of your particular CD-ROM drive.

Once you've highlighted CD Play in the New Button Actions dialog box, and have clicked on "Use this NBA", you will see the audio CD remote control panel. Use the controls to set the starting point and ending point of the sequence you'd like to play, as follows:

Click on "Play" to listen to the CD from the beginning, or use the arrows above "Track" or "Time" to set the CD to a specific track or time (minute, second, frame) position. Click on "Pause" and then "Set Start" to have the starting time set. Click on "Play" to continue listening. You can click on "Pause", then click directly on "Set End" to enter the stopping point of the sequence.

Click on "Try It!" to preview the selection. If the CD is starting too late or too soon, then click on the numbers above "Set Start". (This will set the CD to that point). If you are close to the place that you wanted the CD to begin, then use the arrows above "Time" to adjust the frame numbers. If you are off by a chunk, so to speak, then use the jog shuttle to adjust your position. A big slide will cause the CD to move several minutes, while a short slide will cause it to move seconds.

Be sure to click on "Set Start" again, to set the new starting point. Click on "Try It!". To save your selection, click on "Keep".

Play

Plays the CD. Once you click on "Play", the button changes to "Pause".

Eject

Ejects the CD from the drive.

Set Start

Enters the starting point of your selection. Clicking on the number above this button moves the CD to that position.

Set End

Enters the ending point of your selection. Clicking on the number above this button moves the CD to that position

Position Adjust

Use the jog shuttle to get around the CD.

Try It

Clicking here lets you preview your selection.

Keep

Click here to save the selection.

Options

Displays other neat CD related functions! You can enter track or absolute time numbers manually here. You can also create buttons on cards which will eject a CD, pause it, resume it, stop it, reset it, or repeat the last-played sequence.

BlabberMouth NBA

Using this NBA, your computer will read the text in a text object if you have Speech Manager installed on your Mac! You can also type in the name of a text object, and the text within that particular text container will be read. This works very well on the "A/V" Macintoshes as well!

Changing the Sample Sounds

You may wish to change the "Sample" sounds that come built-in with HyperStudio. These Sample sounds can be accessed by clicking on "Samples" in the Tape deck when playing a sound from a Button or Object. (screen shot of Tape deck with "Samples" checked and sample sounds showing in the window here.)

To change the sample sounds, find the HS Sample Library stack in the HyperStudio folder and simply add or delete buttons with the sounds you wish to this stack.

Chapter 8
Animation

Path Based Animation

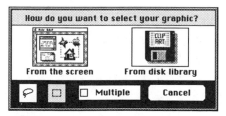

▲▲▲
Animator lets you choose your graphic from either a picture file from disk, or directly from the current card.

To create a path-based animation in HyperStudio, you first need to Add a Button... in the Objects menu. When you get to the Actions window, select New Button Actions from Things To Do:. Click on "Animator" in the New Button Actions window.

Animator allows you to select an area of the screen to animate. Unlike HyperStudio's built-in frame animation (which displays several different frames in rapid succession to give the illusion of movement), with the Animator, you specify a path for a still object to follow.

Using Animator

To use Animator, select it from the list of NBAs and then click "Use this NBA..." You will be returned to the current card, and the dialog box shown to the left will appear, asking where you wish to get the animated graphic. You can animate something currently on the screen, or select something from a clip-art file on disk.

If you select "From disk library," the standard file dialog will appear, prompting you to locate a clip-art file. Additionally, you may choose the tool you wish to use when selecting a graphic to be animated: either Selector tool or the Lasso tool. Note that the Lasso tool will always ignore the outside color, and will "mask out" any colors inside the image that match the outside color. (In other words, if you lasso a doughnut, the background will show through the hole in the middle.) However, later on you can deselect the "This color is invisible" option so that all colors will appear in the graphic image that you lasso without having the graphic image actually appear as a box, as it does with a Selector tool.

Your cursor will have changed to either a crosshair or lasso (depending on the tool that you selected), and you may select an area of the screen. (At this point, you may also press the TAB key to switch between the Lasso and the Selector tools.)

After selecting an area, you'll see the current card. You'll notice that the cursor has

The Animator's control dialog makes it easy to customize your path-animation!
▼▼▼

Animator	Animation Graphic
Roger Wagner Publishing	
Playback rate: 6 (frames/sec.)	
Repeat count: 1	
Record rate: 6 (frames/sec.)	

☒ This is transparent ☐ Loop back... ☐ Can't interrupt
☐ Hide background on 1st frame... ☐ Draw multiple
☐ Hide graphic on last frame ☒ Float over objects

[Path ▼] [Graphic ▼] [Playback] [Cancel] [OK]

changed from a crosshair to the graphic image you selected.

Now you need to determine where on the screen you wish your animation to start. Unless you tell it to do otherwise, any animation sequences you create with Animator will later play in front of the card's background and any objects on the card, (including graphic objects).

To define the animation path, hold down the mouse button and drag. As soon as you hold down the mouse button, the movements are being recorded. When you are finished defining the animation path, release the mouse button. Animator's window will appear, which offers you several options for controlling your animation.

Cel Animation

HyperStudio has the ability to create animation files (internally) on the fly, so that you can make new animations in HyperStudio without having to own any other program.

To add an animation, click "Play animation…" in the Actions window under Things To Do. HyperStudio will present you with the standard file dialog where you can select either a PICS movie file or clip art.

Creating A Cel Animation

If you select a clip art file, HyperStudio will assume that you wish to build an animation from a series of pictures stored on disk that end with consecutive numbers. For example, if you select a file named Bird.1, HyperStudio will assume that you want to build an animation from the frames stored in the files Bird.1, Bird.2, Bird.3, and so on.

Therefore, you will need to have created screen shots with consecutively numbered names before you choose "Play animation". Let's say you wanted to animate a growing plant. Draw the first image on a card, and then choose "Export Screen..." from the File menu, saving it as Plant.1. Then change the image on that same card a little, and save that screen as Plant.2. Continue this process until you've created your series of images on the disk.

After selecting a file, you will see a similar window as you see when you add clip art. Use the scroll bars to see all the art on the screen. To see other clip art files, click the "Get another picture..." button. You may open any PICT, TIFF, EPS, Mac Paint, or any standard Apple IIGS format or 320- or 640-mode, Super Hi-Res picture.

Select your animation's clip art with the Selector tool, creating the "window" that your animation will appear in during the playback. To show HyperStudio where you want your animation to appear during its entire animation cycle, you must make the dotted box as large as is necessary to contain your animation. If your box is too small, part of your animation won't show! Don't make the animation window any larger than necessary, though since the window will cover up everything it plays over.

TIP

- You don't actually need the period for the names, but it does help avoid accidentally putting extra spaces in the name which would confuse HyperStudio in its ordering process.

- The numbers don't actually have to be continuous. Bird 10, Bird 20, Bird 30, would work just as well. In addition, you could then easily insert a frame if you felt it necessary.

If you make a mistake while selecting a graphic or sizing the animation window, simply try again. When you have selected an image, click "OK" or press Return to continue.

At this point, the add clip art window will disappear and the current card will reappear, with your selected image and your animation window floating in the middle of the current card. Put the mouse pointer over the middle of the image and drag the image to wherever you want.

Click outside the rectangle or press Return when you have everything in place as you like it. You then see the Animation dialog box, pictured below. (If the graphic you specified is part of a numbered series of frames, HyperStudio will generate the animation before showing the Animation dialog box.)

The Animation dialog box has many features from which to choose.

Play

The speed is counted in 60ths of a second and controls how fast the animation runs. A value of 30 would tell HyperStudio to show two frames per second. For general purposes, you can consider the rate values of 5, 15, and 30 to be similar to fast, medium, and slow, respectively.

Repeat count

The "Repeat count" value controls how many times the sequence repeats itself—enter "1" to have the animation play just once, or "0" to have the animation play forever.

Try it

Clicking this button will show the top left part of the animation window in the Preview Window.

Position

Clicking this button will allow you to move the graphic and the animation window.

Show first frame

Clicking this box will show the first frame of your animation on the screen when its card is accessed.

Erase when done

Clicking this box will erase the graphic when the animation is finished.

Get another animation...

Clicking this button will return you to the standard file dialog and allow you to choose another PICS movie or clip art file.

Chapter 9
QuickTime™

Using QuickTime Movies

QuickTime movies can either be played or created from within HyperStudio. Objects —Buttons, Text Objects, Graphic Objects and cards—can play QuickTime movies.

In order to use Apple's QuickTime technology, make sure that you have the QuickTime extension in your System folder before beginning.

To make QuickTime movies, you must have a video digitizer and a video source connected to your computer, otherwise you can play QuickTime movie files that already exist.

Playing A QuickTime Movie

To play a QuickTime movie, choose Play a Movie or Video... under "Things to do" in the Actions window when adding actions to a card, button or other object.. Make your choice of where to find your QuickTime movie in the Video/Movie Source window. You can click next to either "Disk file (QuickTime movies)" if you already have a QuickTime movie on file to use or you may click "Video (make your own movie)" if you have a video digitizer connected to your computer. This option will allow you to make a QuickTime movie on the fly from within HyperStudio.

After you choose either to make your own movie or to use an existing QuickTime movie file, you will then see the first frame of the movie on your card. This is the window the movie will show in. You may move the box anywhere on the screen you'd like. Click inside the movie and drag it to the location you want it to play on your card. You can also resize the box, but this may cause the movie to play more slowly. Click outside the movie to call up the QuickTime Movies dialog box. You can make choices as to how your movie will look when played as follows:

Erase when done: This will cause the movie to disappear from the card once it has been played.

Play over objects: You have the choice of showing the movie over an object, or from

The **Video / Movie Source** dialog.
▼▼▼

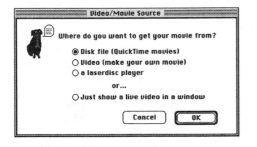

behind an object. An interesting effect is playing the movie from behind a graphic object. When you add an abject with the lasso tool, the color surrounding the object is transparent in all cases where it appears in that graphic. So if you add a TV as a graphic object, and the screen of the TV is transparent (as a doughnut, because the color surrounding the TV is the same as the screen color), then the QuickTime movie can be played through this hole. In this case, you would not choose to Play over objects.

Use movie controller: You can have a slider at the bottom of the QuickTime movie which will give the user control over playing the movie.

Loop movie: Have the movie play continuously until you leave the card or click the mouse.

Show first frame: The first frame of the movie can be on the card before you click the button to play the movie. If you choose this option, and you have a controller bar, you can double-click on the first frame to start the movie.

Try It: Shows how your movie looks before clicking OK.

Position: Click this to reposition your movie on the card.

Get another movie…: Allows you to select a different QuickTime movie file.

Making Your Own Movies

You can make your own QuickTime movies right in HyperStudio provided that you have a video digitizer and a video source connected to your computer.

To do this, choose Play a Movie or Video… under Things to do in the Actions window when adding actions to a card, button or other object. Click next to "Video (make your own movie)" in the Video/Movie Source window. This will take you to the New Movie dialog box where you will have a choice of buttons with video and sound options and a Record button. Simply press Record to make your movie. Click OK when finished.

▲▲▲
You are given a choice of the source for your movie.

You will then see the first frame of the movie on your card. This is the window the movie will show in. You may move the box anywhere on the screen you'd like. Click inside the movie and drag it to the location you want it to play on your card. If you resize the box, the movie will play more slowly. Click outside the movie to call up the QuickTime Movies dialog box. You can make choices as to how your movie will look when played here:

Erase when done: This will cause the movie to disappear from the card once it has been played.

Play over objects: You have the choice of showing the movie over an object, or from behind an object. An interesting effect is playing the movie from behind a graphic object. When you add an abject with the lasso tool, the color surrounding the object is transparent in all cases where it appears in that graphic. So if you add a TV as a graphic object, and the screen of the TV is transparent (as a doughnut, because the color surrounding the TV is the same as the screen color), then the QuickTime movie can be played through this hole. In this case, you would not choose to Play over objects.

Use movie controller: You can have a slider at the bottom of the QuickTime movie which will give the user control over playing the movie.

Loop movie: Have the movie play continuously until you leave the card or click the mouse.

Show first frame: The first frame of the movie can be on the card before you click the button to play the movie. If you choose this option, and you have a controller bar, you can double-click on the first frame to start the movie.

Try It: Shows how your movie looks before clicking OK.

Position: Click this to reposition your movie on the card.

Get another movie...: Allows you to select a different QuickTime movie file.

TIP

Better Image Quality

- Most QuickTime movies are created with 256-colors or more. If you play a 256-color movie in a 16 color stack, the movie may be slower. In order to play a QuickTime at it's optimum speed and best colors in HyperStudio, make sure your stack is set to display 256 colors.

Editing QuickTime movies

QuickTime movies can be edited outside of HyperStudio extensively using a QuickTime movie editing software package. There are many such packages available for the Macintosh. Simple QuickTime movie editing may be done in a program such as Simple Player, which also plays QuickTime movies outside of HyperStudio.

Editing a QuickTime movie from within HyperStudio is limited to the choices you have when creating or adding a movie to a card, button or other object. Changes to the movie can be made by editing the object which plays it with the edit tools in the top portion of the Tool palette.

Playing Movies In Irregular Shapes

Playing a QuickTime movie behind a piece of clip art, such as a TV, can make the movie appear as if it is playing on the TV screen!

To do this, first add a piece of clip art by choosing Add Clip Art from the File menu. Select the clip art in the Clip Art window and click OK. Make sure the area that you want your movie to show through is the same color as the background of your card. Go to the File menu and Export Screen. Erase your card and go the Objects menu and Add a Graphic Object... Choose your exported screen file and lasso the clip art. Click OK in the Graphic Appearance window. Add a Button and select Play a Video or Movie... in the Actions window under Things To Do. Choose the QuickTime movie you wish to play and when you click the button on your card, you'll see the movie play through your TV screen or any other clip art. (please find out how to do this in more detail in the HyperStudio Tutorial)

Chapter 10
Windows

HyperStudio and Windows

This section explains the similarities of HyperStudio for Macintosh with that of the Windows version.

Moving Your Stacks Back and Forth

It is entirely possible to move your HyperStudio stacks back and forth from a Macintosh to a PC running Windows. Your stacks are computer-independent and loading a stack on either computer will be transparent as each computer will recognize the other's HyperStudio stacks. Imagine starting a project in the Macintosh at school, then taking the project home and finishing it in Windows on a PC, and vice-versa!

There are some things you need to be aware of when doing this, however, and certain incompatibilities will change as new versions of the HyperStudio software on both computers continue to be updated and developed.

In order to move your stacks back and forth from a Macintosh to a PC, you must have the HyperStudio program version for each computer and the proper version installed on the computers to be used. When using the Windows version of HyperStudio, you must be running Windows 3.1 or better on your PC. Other considerations include:

Mac/Windows Filenames & Pathnames

It is important to follow Windows guidelines for filenames and pathnames when creating stacks on the Macintosh that you expect to use on the PC. As an example, one consideration you must make is that Macintosh filenames and pathnames can be 32 characters long while PC filenames and pathnames must be no longer than 8 characters. There are other considerations here that may require you to consult your PC user's guide.

Mac/Windows Fonts

Using the same TrueType fonts on both computers will ensure that the fonts you use in your stacks will be displayed on both the Macintosh and the PC. This is especially critical with the fonts used in Text Objects, which can change from computer to computer depending on which fonts reside on the computers used.

Mac/Windows NBAs

Any New Button Actions (NBAs) you use on one computer will not work when moving your stack back and forth unless you have a matching NBA on the other computer. As time goes on, "matching" NBAs will be developed for both the Macintosh and the PC running Windows.

Mac/Windows Sounds

The sounds used in your stacks to be moved back and forth from your Macintosh to your PC running Windows, must be "uncompressed" sounds in order for them to translate well on the PC.

Mac/Windows and HyperStudio Macintosh 3.0 Features

Certain HyperStudio for the Macintosh version 3.0 features such as Object Actions and HyperText are not available on the HyperStudio Windows version of the software at this time. All features incorporated into the Macintosh version of HyperStudio, however, are planned to be included in future releases of the Windows version of HyperStudio.

Chapter 11
Internet

HyperStudio has built-in Internet access! The tools to bring Internet data right into your stacks are a part of the total HyperStudio package. The MediaLinker application and the MacWebPage NBA make it possible to search the Internet for text, graphics, sounds and more to be used in your stacks. For example, providing you have an open connection to the Internet, a reference file, called a MediaLink (created with MediaLinker), can fetch the file you want from the Internet, while working on your stack by simply adding clip art, text or a sound, etc. in the usual ways within HyperStudio. The MacWebPage NBA allows you to access the World Wide Web on the Internet through the MacWeb program.

MediaLinker

The "MediaLinker" program (located in the HS Internet folder on your CD), creates Internet reference files called "MediaLinks" which can be accessed from within HyperStudio just as any other text, graphic or sound file can be brought into a stack. Sample MediaLinks can be found on your HyperStudio CD located in the HS Internet folder.

MediaLinker is part navigational tool, part organizer, and part stepping stone. If you use the Internet then you know it is not the most friendly place to wander. Even with excellent tools such as NetScape, Mosaic, NewsWatcher, Anarchie or TurboGopher, making the most of the resources on the Internet is still reserved for the technically inclined. Most creative types would not rather delve into the world of URL's and HTML in an effort to communicate.

Rather than requiring people to write URL's as a reference to a particular resource, MediaLinker generates another kind of reference - a MediaLink - which can include preview images, preview sounds, a description, as well as how to obtain the resource. All this information about the resource is kept in a small file, right on your hard drive.

You can then organize these MediaLink files any way you like. For example, you could have a folder of "wildlife" MediaLinks on your disk, taking up no more than 200k of disk space, but the MediaLinks could refer you to many different servers holding several gigabytes of images, text, etc. out on the Internet.

Later, in HyperStudio, these MediaLinks can be included in stacks, and if the stack is viewed while connected to the Internet, The resource will be retrieved and presented to the viewer.

This is Where MediaLinker comes in, it's the tool used to build libraries of interesting MediaLinks to resources on the Internet.

MediaLinker requires a Macintosh running System 7.0 or later with 1 MB of memory and a hard drive. MediaLinker will run in native PowerPC mode on Power Macintoshes and in M68k mode on 68k Macintoshes.

The Macintosh must be connected to the Internet through a SLIP, PPP or a gateway connection. MacTCP must be properly installed and configured. As MediaLinker provides resource browsing, it requires a continuous connection to the Internet during use.

MediaLinker does not support serial dial-up communications or terminal emulation. It is unlikely that these features will be added in the future.

MacWebPage NBA

The MacWebPage New Button Action (NBA) works with the MacWeb program and allows HyperStudio to "talk" to this World Wide Web browser. This NBA tells MacWeb to go to certain places on the Web to find what you want while in a HyperStudio stack. You must have System 7.0 or later, the MacWeb program and MacTCP installed and an open connection to the Internet while accessing the MacWebPage NBA.

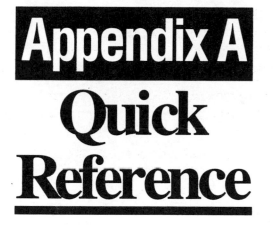

This appendix provides a quick overview of HyperStudio's menus, dialogs and keyboard shortcuts. You may find yourself refering to this appendix quite often, once you have become familiar with HyperStudio. This appendix is devided into two sections: Keyboard Shortcuts & Menus.

Keyboard Shortcuts

⌘ - A	Add Clip Art		⌘ - P	Print
⌘ - B	Add a Button		⌘ - Q	Quit HyperStudio
⌘ - C	Copy		⌘ - R	Record (in Tape Deck)
⌘ - E	Export Screen		⌘ - S	Save
⌘ - F	Find Text		⌘ - T	Add a Text Object
⌘ - F-Shift *to Find next occurance*			⌘ - V	Paste
⌘ - G	Add a Graphic Object		⌘ - X	Cut
⌘ - H	Home		⌘ - Y	Text Style
⌘ - I	Import Background		⌘ - Z	Undo
⌘ - J	Jump to Card		⌘ - 1	First Card
⌘ - K	Standard Colors		⌘ - 9	Last Card
⌘ - L	Hypertext Link		⌘ - ~	Back
⌘ - M	Menu Bar (hide or show)		⌘ - >	Next Card
⌘ - N	New Card		⌘ - <	Previous Card
⌘ - O	Open Stack		⌘ - ;	Preferences

Additional Keyboard Shortcuts:

⌘ - +:	Bring object forward one level.
⌘ - -:	Send object farther one level.
Shift-⌘- +:	Bring object to front.
Shift-⌘- -:	Send object to back.
Shift-Tab:	Toggle between Browse & Arrow tool.
Shift-Control-Tab:	To get to the Selector Tool.
Option-Drag:	On selection or object to make a copy.
Option-⌘:	To see outline of all invisible buttons.

TIP

Using Keyboard Shortcuts

- To use a keyboard shortcut, first press and hold the Command key (the one with the ⌘ symbol) and then press on the letter. For example: to Find Text, press and hold the ⌘ key and then press the key with the letter "F".

File

New Stack	
Open Stack...	⌘O
Save Stack	⌘S
Save Stack As...	
Import Background...	⌘I
Export Screen...	⌘E
Add Clip Art...	⌘A
Page Setup...	
Print...	⌘P
Print to Video...	
Quit HyperStudio	⌘Q

- **Creates** a new stack.
- **Opens an existing stack** from your hard drive or a floppy disk.
- **Saves your stack** on disk without a dialog.
- **Saves your stack for the first time** displaying the "Save As" dialog.

- **Loads a picture** from an art file which will cover the entire card.
- **Saves the current screen** as an art file for later use as a background or as clip art.
- **Adds a piece of art** and pastes it to your background.

- **Prints** the cards in the stack to a printer.
- Allows you to do a "slide show" of your stack. Use your VCR to record it!

Type the name of your stack here.

⚠ This stack was changed, do you want to save it?

[Don't Save]   [Cancel]   [Save]

When you quit HyperStudio, choose New Stack, or open another stack, you will be reminded to save the current stack if you haven't already done so.

Print to Video

○ Print until escape key pressed
◉ Print all cards automatically
   Pause [5] seconds between cards

[Cancel]   [Start]

Card printing
◉ Current card   ◉ One card per page
○ All cards   ○ Two cards per page
                    ○ Four cards per page

Number of pages to be printed: 1

[Cancel]   [OK]

- **Quits** the HyperStudio application.

Edit

Undo	⌘Z
Cut	⌘H
Copy	⌘C
Paste text	⌘U
Clear	
New Card	⌘N
Ready Made Cards	▶
Delete Card	
Cut Card	
Copy Card	
Edit this Object...	
Effects	▶
Erase Background...	
Preferences	⌘;

- **Undo** is used when you make a mistake or change your mind about something. Works on the most recent (last) change you made.

- **New Card** adds one new card to your stack, at the position right after the current one.

- Inserts a card from the **Ready Made Cards** folder. Use this feature to create your own HyperStudio card templates!

- **Permanently removes** the current card.

- Removes the current card and places it on the **clipboard**. You can then paste the card elsewhere in the stack or a different stack.

- Makes a **copy** of the current card and places it on the clipboard for later pasting.

- **Cut:** Before you Cut something which you plan to Paste, you must select it first. Art is selected with the ▭, or the ⌀, while Buttons, Text Objects and Graphic Objects are selected with the Pointer tool ▶. Once you Cut something it waits on the clipboard to be pasted.

- **Copy** works the same way as Cut, except the original is left on the screen.

- **Paste** takes whatever was Copied or Cut earlier and places it in a new place.

- **Clear** works like Cut, but whatever was Cleared does not wait on the clipboard.

- Select the **object** you want to edit with the pointer tool, then choose this option.

- Changes the **background** color of a card & erases the background.

- **Replaces** or **Exchanges** two different colors within a selected area.

- Paints a **gradient fill** within a selected area.

- Sets the **Preferences** of the current stack.

Flip Sideways
Flip Upside Down
Scale & Rotate...
Replace Colors...
Gradients...

Replace/Exchange Colors

Scale & Rotate

Scale factor
120 %

Rotation angle
45 °
● Clockwise
○ Counter-clockwise

- Once you have selected an area, you can resize it and/or rotate it. Note that *Rotate* works only with the tool, while *Scale* works with ▭, ○ and the ⌀ tools.

Example of the original made 20% larger & rotated 45 degrees clockwise.

Original ————————▶ **Result**

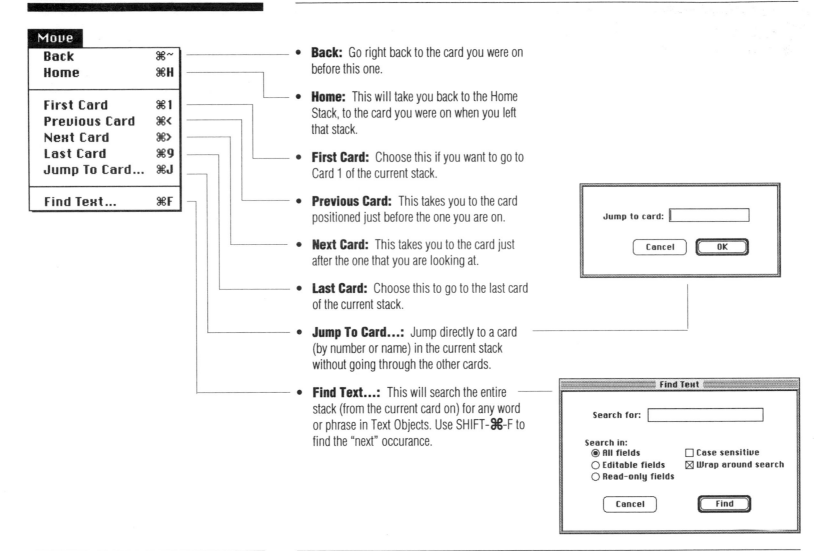

Move

Back	⌘~
Home	⌘H
First Card	⌘1
Previous Card	⌘<
Next Card	⌘>
Last Card	⌘9
Jump To Card...	⌘J
Find Text...	⌘F

- **Back:** Go right back to the card you were on before this one.

- **Home:** This will take you back to the Home Stack, to the card you were on when you left that stack.

- **First Card:** Choose this if you want to go to Card 1 of the current stack.

- **Previous Card:** This takes you to the card positioned just before the one you are on.

- **Next Card:** This takes you to the card just after the one that you are looking at.

- **Last Card:** Choose this to go to the last card of the current stack.

- **Jump To Card...:** Jump directly to a card (by number or name) in the current stack without going through the other cards.

- **Find Text...:** This will search the entire stack (from the current card on) for any word or phrase in Text Objects. Use SHIFT-⌘-F to find the "next" occurance.

Jump to card: [ ]

Cancel   OK

Find Text

Search for: [ ]

Search in:
- ⦿ **All fields**   ☐ **Case sensitive**
- ○ **Editable fields**   ☒ **Wrap around search**
- ○ **Read-only fields**

Cancel   Find

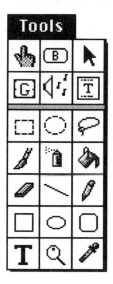

Tools

Edit Tools

Paint Tools

Browse Tool	Button Edit Tool	Arrow Tool
Graphic Edit Tool	Sound Edit Tool	Text Edit Tool
Rectangle Selector	Circle Selector	Lasso
Paintbrush	Spraypaint Tool	Fill Tool
Eraser	Line Tool	Pencil
Rectangle Tool	Oval Tool	Rounded Rectangle Tool
Text Tool	Magnifying Glass	Eye Dropper

Tool Description	Double-clicking object	Modifiers
Browse Tool Used to activate objects with attached actions. This tool is used for "playing back" your stack.	Use "ignore extra mouse clicks" option in the preferences dialog to ignore double-clicks.	• Using Shift-Tab toggles between the Browse tool and the Arrow tool.
Button Edit Tool Use for editing or moving an existing button.	Double-clicking a button displays the Button Appearance dialog.	• Double-clicking a button with the Command key pressed bypasses the Button Appearance dialog and goes directly to the Actions dialog. • While moving a button, press the Shift key to restrain movement to a vertical or horizontal direction. • While moving a button, press the Option key to duplicate the button.
Arrow Tool Used to edit or move buttons, text objects or graphic objects. Also referred to as the "pointer" tool.	Double-clicking an object displays that particular object's information dialog.	• Using Shift-Tab toggles between the Browse tool and the Arrow tool. • Double-clicking a button with the Command key pressed bypasses the button appearance dialog and goes directly to the Actions dialog. • While moving an object, press the Shift key to constrain movement to a vertical or horizontal direction. • While moving an object, press the Option key to duplicate the object.

Tool Description	Double-clicking object	Modifiers
Graphic Edit Tool [G] Used for editing or moving graphic objects.	Double-clicking a graphic object displays the Graphic Appearance dialog.	• No change
Sound Edit Tool Used for editing only buttons that contain sounds.	Double-clicking a button displays the Button Appearance dialog.	• No change
Text Edit Tool [T] Used for editing or moving text objects.	Double-clicking a text object displays the Text Appearance dialog.	• No change

Tool Description	Double-clicking	Modifiers
Rectangle Selector — Lets you capture a rectangular area. Used to copy, cut, delete, move, flip, rotate or resize a selected area of the background.	Entire background is selected within a rectangular shape. The upper left corner determines the color that will remain when the selection is moved or deleted.	• Resize the selected area by grabbing near the corner and dragging the mouse. • Hold down the Option key while dragging the mouse to create a copy without removing the original. If "Draw multiple" is checked while Option-dragging, multiple copies will trail behind the mouse path. • Press Shift-Control-Tab to switch between the Selector and Browse modes.
Circle Selector — Lets you capture an oval or circular area. Used to copy, cut, delete, move or resize a selected area of the background.	The background is selected within an oval shape.	• Hold down the Option key while dragging the mouse to create a copy without removing the original. • If "Draw multiple" is checked while Option-dragging, multiple copies will trail behind the mouse path.
Lasso — Selects an irregular shape on the card's background. Used to copy, cut, delete or move a selected area of the background.	Entire background is selected with the most upper-left corner determining the "invisible" or "see-through" color.	• Once an area is selected, hold down the Option key while dragging the mouse to create a copy without removing the original. If "Draw multiple" is checked while Option-dragging, multiple copies will trail behind the mouse path. • Hold the Option key down while clicking within an area to do an "expanding lasso". • Hold the ⌘ key down while selecting an area to do a "pencil" lasso.

Tool Description	Double-clicking	Modifiers
Paintbrush Draw freehand using one of many different brush shapes. Paints with the currently selected color or pattern.	Displays brush shape dialog. Cancel OK	• Select the color or pattern from the Colors menu. • Hold down the Shift key while dragging for perfectly straight horizontal or vertical lines. • Select "Brush Shape" from the Options menu to change the brush shape.
Spraypaint Tool Scatters tiny dots of the currently selected color or pattern.	No action.	• Select the color or pattern from the Colors menu. • Hold down the Shift key while dragging for perfectly straight horizontal or vertical lines.
Fill Tool Fills a closed shape with the currently selected color or pattern.	No action.	• Select the color or pattern from the Colors menu.

Tool Description	Double-clicking	Modifiers
Eraser Erases portions of the background with the current background color or pattern.	Displays this dialog, and then erases the entire background. Choose the background color: Cancel OK	• Select "Eraser Color..." from the Options menu to set the color or pattern to erase with. • Hold down the Shift key while dragging for perfectly straight horizontal or vertical lines.
Line Tool Draws straight lines with the current color or pattern, and the current line size.	Allows you to specify a new line size (thickness). Cancel OK	• Select "Line Size..." from the Options menu to change the line thickness. • Select the color or pattern from the Colors menu. • Select "Draw Multiple" from the Options menu to draw repeat images as you drag the mouse. • Select "Draw Centered" from the Options menu to draw from the center instead of the end. • Select "Brush Shape" from the Options menu to change the brush shape. • Hold down the Shift key while dragging to constrain the tool to 45 degree increments.
Pencil Draws freehand shapes with the current color or pattern.	Zooms in to the Magnifier mode.	• Select the color or pattern from the Colors menu. • Hold down the Shift key while dragging for perfectly straight horizontal or vertical lines. • Hold the Command key while clicking on a color to change to the color you clicked on.

Tool Description	Double-clicking	Modifiers
Rectangle Tool Draws rectangles and squares with the current color or pattern.	Toggles the drawing mode: filled or empty.	• Select "Draw Filled" from the Options menu to draw solid shapes as you drag the mouse. • Select the color or pattern from the Colors menu. • Select "Draw Multiple" from the Options menu to draw repeat images as you drag the mouse. • Select "Draw Centered" from the Options menu to draw from the center instead of the end. • Hold down the Shift key while dragging to draw squares instead of rectangles.
Oval Tool Draws ovals or circles with the current color or pattern.	Toggles the drawing mode: filled or empty.	• Select the color or pattern from the Colors menu. • Select "Draw Filled" from the Options menu to draw solid shapes as you drag the mouse. • Select "Draw Multiple" from the Options menu to draw repeat images as you drag the mouse. • Select "Draw Centered" from the Options menu to draw from the center instead of the end. • Hold down the Shift key while dragging to draw circles instead of ovals.
Rounded Rectangle Tool Draws rectangles and squares that have rounded corners with the current color or pattern.	Toggles the drawing mode: filled or empty.	• Select the color or pattern from the Colors menu. • Select "Draw Filled" from the Options menu to draw solid shapes as you drag the mouse. • Select "Draw Multiple" from the Options menu to draw repeat images as you drag the mouse. • Select "Draw Centered" from the Options menu to draw from the center instead of the end. • Hold down the Shift key while dragging to draw rounded squares instead of rounded rectangles.

Tool Description	Double-clicking	Modifiers
Text Tool Paints text onto the background with the current color and the current text style.	Calls up the text style dialog. *[Text Style dialog box showing fonts: Souvenir, Spaghetti Western, SteelWolf-Medium, Symbol, Tekton, Tekton Bold; styles: Plain, Bold, Italic, Underline, Outline, Shadow, Condensed, Extended; Size: 18; Text Color palette; quote "Imagination is more important than knowledge. - Albert Einstein"; Cancel / OK]*	• Select the text style and color from the Options menu. • Select the color of the text by choosing a color from the color palette.
Magnifying Glass Zooms in for a closer view of the background.	Zooms into the "Fat Bits" or magnifier mode for a close up view of the background.	• Press the Escape key to return to 100% magnification. • With the pencil tool selected, hold down the Command key and click to select the color under the cursor. • Hold down the Option key and drag the mouse to scroll the screen.
Eye Dropper Click on a color on the background to change your current painting color.	No Action	• To change the erasor color, instead of the foreground color, hold down the Option key while clicking on the background.

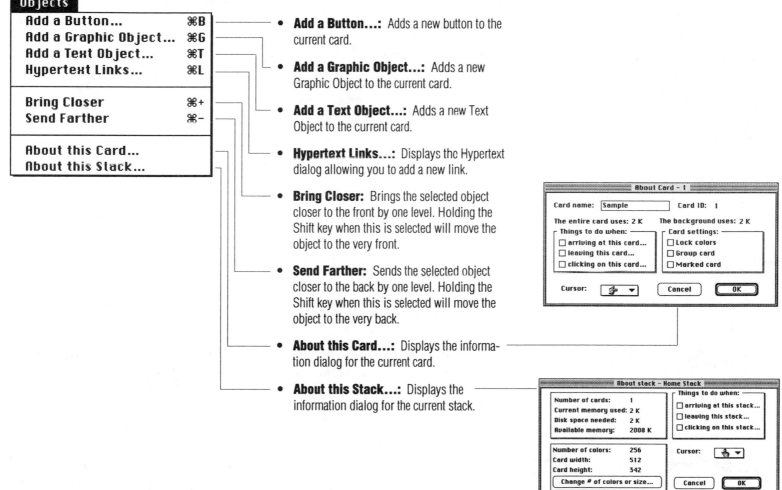

Objects

Add a Button...	⌘B
Add a Graphic Object...	⌘G
Add a Text Object...	⌘T
Hypertext Links...	⌘L
Bring Closer	⌘+
Send Farther	⌘–
About this Card...	
About this Stack...	

- **Add a Button...:** Adds a new button to the current card.

- **Add a Graphic Object...:** Adds a new Graphic Object to the current card.

- **Add a Text Object...:** Adds a new Text Object to the current card.

- **Hypertext Links...:** Displays thc Hypertext dialog allowing you to add a new link.

- **Bring Closer:** Brings the selected object closer to the front by one level. Holding the Shift key when this is selected will move the object to the very front.

- **Send Farther:** Sends the selected object closer to the back by one level. Holding the Shift key when this is selected will move the object to the very back.

- **About this Card...:** Displays the information dialog for the current card.

- **About this Stack...:** Displays the information dialog for the current stack.

About Card - 1

Card name: Sample   Card ID: 1

The entire card uses: 2 K   The background uses: 2 K

Things to do when:
- ☐ arriving at this card...
- ☐ leaving this card...
- ☐ clicking on this card...

Card settings:
- ☐ Lock colors
- ☐ Group card
- ☐ Marked card

Cursor: [☞ ▼]   Cancel   OK

About stack - Home Stack

Number of cards: 1
Current memory used: 2 K
Disk space needed: 2 K
Available memory: 2008 K

Number of colors: 256
Card width: 512
Card height: 342

[Change # of colors or size...]

Things to do when:
- ☐ arriving at this stack...
- ☐ leaving this stack...
- ☐ clicking on this stack...

Cursor: [✋ ▼]

Cancel   OK

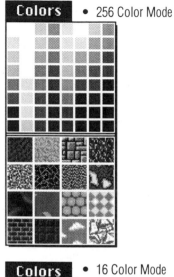

• 256 Color Mode

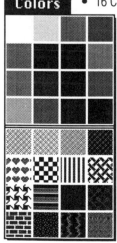

• 16 Color Mode

The Colors palette can be "torn off" from the menu bar. This makes it easy to select colors and patterns.

- To tear off the menu, click on the Colors menu and drag the mouse down and to the left, as illustrated below.
- Release the mouse to place the menu.
- Colors and patterns can then be selected simply by clicking on the color or pattern square of your choice.

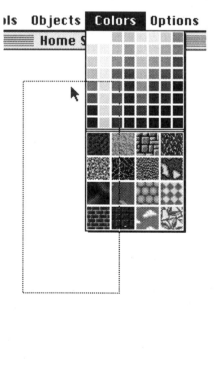

After the color palette has been torn off the menu bar, several options become available:

- Click here to close (put away) the color palette.
- Click and drag on the gray bar to move the color palette to a new location on the screen.

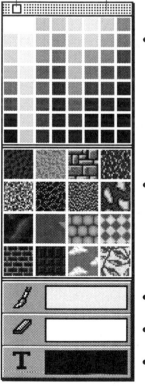

- Click on a color square to paint with that color. Or, double-click any one of the color squares to make it a new color.

- Click on a pattern square to paint with the pattern.

- This shows the current paint color or pattern
- This shows the current eraser color or pattern.
- This shows the current Text color.

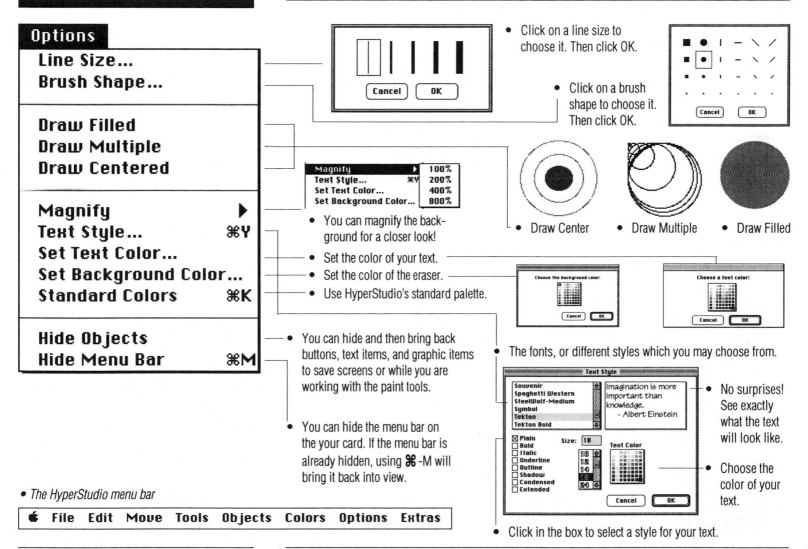

Options

Line Size...
Brush Shape...

Draw Filled
Draw Multiple
Draw Centered

Magnify ▶
Text Style... ⌘Y
Set Text Color...
Set Background Color...
Standard Colors ⌘K

Hide Objects
Hide Menu Bar ⌘M

- Click on a line size to choose it. Then click OK.

- Click on a brush shape to choose it. Then click OK.

Magnify ▶ 100%
Text Style... ⌘Y 200%
Set Text Color... 400%
Set Background Color... 800%

- You can magnify the background for a closer look!
- Set the color of your text.
- Set the color of the eraser.
- Use HyperStudio's standard palette.

- Draw Center - Draw Multiple - Draw Filled

Choose the background color: Choose a text color:

Cancel OK   Cancel OK

- You can hide and then bring back buttons, text items, and graphic items to save screens or while you are working with the paint tools.

- You can hide the menu bar on the your card. If the menu bar is already hidden, using ⌘-M will bring it back into view.

- *The HyperStudio menu bar*

 🍎 File Edit Move Tools Objects Colors Options Extras

- The fonts, or different styles which you may choose from.

Text Style

Souvenir
Spaghetti Western
SteelWolf-Medium
Symbol
Tekton
Tekton Bold

Imagination is more important than knowledge.
- Albert Einstein

☒ Plain   Size: 18
☐ Bold
☐ Italic
☐ Underline   10
☐ Outline   12
☐ Shadow   14
☐ Condensed   18
☐ Extended   24

Text Color

Cancel OK

- No surprises! See exactly what the text will look like.

- Choose the color of your text.

- Click in the box to select a style for your text.

Actions dialog detail

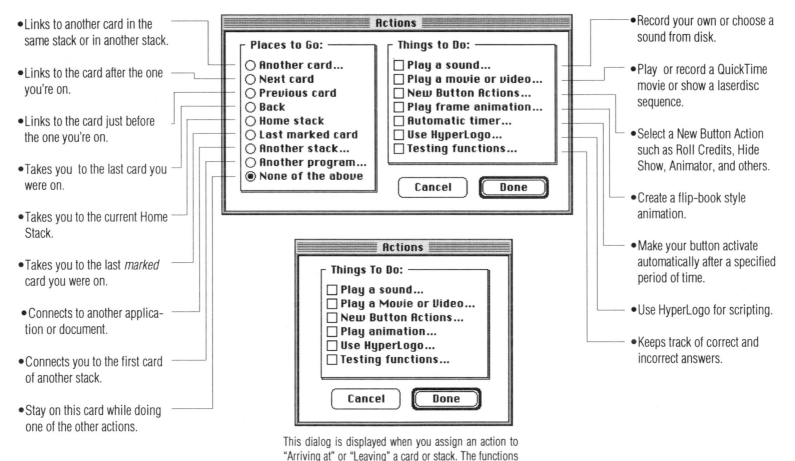

- Links to another card in the same stack or in another stack.
- Links to the card after the one you're on.
- Links to the card just before the one you're on.
- Takes you to the last card you were on.
- Takes you to the current Home Stack.
- Takes you to the last *marked* card you were on.
- Connects to another application or document.
- Connects you to the first card of another stack.
- Stay on this card while doing one of the other actions.

Actions

Places to Go:
- ○ Another card...
- ○ Next card
- ○ Previous card
- ○ Back
- ○ Home stack
- ○ Last marked card
- ○ Another stack...
- ○ Another program...
- ● None of the above

Things to Do:
- ☐ Play a sound...
- ☐ Play a movie or video...
- ☐ New Button Actions...
- ☐ Play frame animation...
- ☐ Automatic timer...
- ☐ Use HyperLogo...
- ☐ Testing functions...

[Cancel] [**Done**]

- Record your own or choose a sound from disk.
- Play or record a QuickTime movie or show a laserdisc sequence.
- Select a New Button Action such as Roll Credits, Hide Show, Animator, and others.
- Create a flip-book style animation.
- Make your button activate automatically after a specified period of time.
- Use HyperLogo for scripting.
- Keeps track of correct and incorrect answers.

Actions

Things To Do:
- ☐ Play a sound...
- ☐ Play a Movie or Video...
- ☐ New Button Actions...
- ☐ Play animation...
- ☐ Use HyperLogo...
- ☐ Testing functions...

[Cancel] [**Done**]

This dialog is displayed when you assign an action to "Arriving at" or "Leaving" a card or stack. The functions are exactly the same as above, except that "Places To Go:" and "Automatic Timer..." are not available.

Preferences dialog detail

Edit

Undo Painting	⌘Z
Cut	⌘H
Copy	⌘C
Paste	⌘U
Clear	
New Card	⌘N
Ready Made Cards	▶
Delete Card	
Cut Card	
Copy Card	
Edit this Object...	
Effects	▶
Erase Background...	
Preferences	⌘;

▲▲▲

To get to the Preferences dialog, select *Preferences* from the **Edit** menu, or use ⌘ - ; (⌘ + semi-colon)

Presentation Options

When *Presentation mode* is selected, this dialog appears: ▶ ▶ ▶

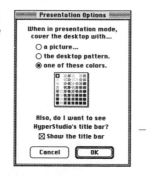

Presentation Options

When in presentation mode, cover the desktop with...

○ a picture...
○ the desktop pattern.
◉ one of these colors.

Also, do I want to see HyperStudio's title bar?
☒ Show the title bar

Cancel | OK

Stack Password

- Set a password for stacks you wish to lock with "Lock stack" checked.
- Other checkboxes will be grayed out.

Lock Stack

- By selecting Lock stack, all menus except File, Edit and Move will become unavailable to the user.

Automatically Save Stack

- Your stack will be saved whenever you quit HyperStudio or open another stack.

Presentation mode

- This allows you to cover the desktop with a color, the desktop pattern, or a picture. It also prevents you from clicking on the desktop!
- Show title bar: It's nice to see the title bar while working on stacks, and hiding it for final presentations.

Preferences

┌ **Stack preferences** ──────────
Stack password: [My Password]
☐ Lock stack...
☐ Show card number with stack name
☐ Turn on Magic Buttons & HyperLinks
☐ Automatically save stack
☐ Presentation mode...
☐ Ignore extra mouse clicks

┌ **Program preferences** ──────────
☒ I'm an experienced HyperStudio user
E-mail address: [   ]

Cancel | OK

Show card with stack name

- Select this if you want the stack name and the card number to appear at the top of your cards.

Turn on Automatic timer & HyperLinks

- This turns on both Automatic timer and HyperLinks, making it easier to edit stacks.

Ignore extra mouse clicks

- This causes HyperStudio to treat a double-click as if it were a single-click.

E-mail address:

- Used for Internet access.

OK & Cancel • Use these to keep (OK) or cancel settings.

I'm an experienced HyperStudio user

- Avoids dialog boxes that explain things when you create a Button or Text Object for the **first** time.
- Controls whether you see **only** sounds or icon files when you add a sound or icon. If you're an experienced user, then you see **all** files which have resources.
- If you're adding a QuickTime movie, and it doesn't match your color level, (you'r⁻ in 16 colors and the movie has more colors), as an experienced user you will be shown the conversion/compression options.
- Allows you to choose the features of Buttons, Text Objects and Graphic Objects. The *features* button is only available to experienced users.

Appendix B

Using HyperStudio With Other Software

HyperStudio is designed to work with many other software packages. It is our goal that HyperStudio be an ideal place to bring together information from many different resources.

The appendix provided information will allow you to integrate text, graphics, sound, and QuickTime movies from other programs into your HyperStudio projects.

HyperStudio can be used with many different programs. We have chosen some of the more popular software titles to illustrate what is possible, but this list is provided as a beginning, not a boundary. Programs covered in this section are:

> **The Print Shop** *Broderbund*
>
> **Kid Pix** *Broderbund*
>
> **The Writing Center** *The Learning Company*
>
> **Grolier's Multimedia Encyclopedia** *Mindscape*
>
> **U. S. Atlas** *Mindscape*
>
> **World Atlas** *Mindscape*
>
> **The Animals** *Mindscape*
>
> **Mammals** *The National Geographic Society*
>
> **Clarisworks** *Claris*
>
> **Hypercard** *Apple Computer*
>
> **Encarta** *Microsoft*

Types of Data

Although there are many different software programs and resources that can be used with HyperStudio, the types of data that you will be retrieving from each are the same. In any of the programs, the things you will want to consider are text, graphics, sound and digital movies.

HyperStudio supports the Mac clipboard, scrapbook, and standard types of data, so in general, if the program's designers provided the information in a standard format, HyperStudio can access it.

In addition, HyperStudio has a number of advanced features that will let you "go inside" other programs, even if the data has not been made readily available, and an additional utility, "PICTify", that is provided in the HyperStudio package will let you capture anything from the screen. At the very least, if you can see it on your computer screen, you'll be able to at least capture it as clip-art.

Following is an overview of each data type, and what you can do to move that type of information from an outside resource to within your HyperStudio project.

On the pages following this overview, you'll find a specific section for each of the programs listed earlier.

NOTE: There is a general process for switching between programs, and moving data using either the clipboard, the Scrapbook Desk Accessory, saving data to disk, or capturing it from the screen. Please be sure to read the "Text" section coming up next, as this will provide information that will be referred to in the sections on the other data types.

Text

Text is one of the most standard data types in computing, with international standards having been established for how it will be stored in any computer, regardless of platform or program.

Assuming you are looking at some text on the screen that you wish to move to HyperStudio, let's look at the general ways to do that which might be possible in any program, depending on its design.

There are four approaches described here, with the following advantages and limitations:

A. Move the text using the clipboard with both programs open at the same time. This requires that you have enough memory to have both programs open. The advantage is that you can easily (and without any particular planning) move back and forth between your resource program and HyperStudio as the mood suits you, grabbing an individual bit of information each time without having to reopen or close either application. The disadvantage is that you can't grab more than one item at a time in the resource application. You've got to move one piece of information at a time, and then go back for the next.

B. Moving the text using the clipboard with only one program open at a time. For those that don't have enough memory to keep both open, you can run one program, grab the text and put it on the clipboard, then quit that and run HyperStudio to paste it. This is the least efficient, because of the time to quit and restart each program. If you're copying more than one piece of data, it's better to use the Scrapbook approach, next.

C. Put multiple data pieces in the Scrapbook desk accessory. Then move back to HyperStudio and paste them as needed. The advantage is that you can stay in the other application for a while, and gather up a collection of data. The disadvantage is that you have to remember to delete the data from the Scrapbook when you're done.

D. Saving data to disk. This is only an option for programs that have an export text feature. The advantage is that if you can only keep one program open at a time, you can grab and export several pieces of data. The disadvantage is that you'll have the working files left on your hard disk until you delete them, although for many users, dragging files to the trash is easier than having to sequentially delete data from the scrapbook.

Here are each of those approaches in detail:

A. Moving the Text Using the Clipboard - Both Programs Open

If you have enough memory on your computer (6mb or more), you may be able to have both the other application and HyperStudio open at the same time. If additionally the program you are using has been well-designed, and the Edit menu is enabled, any text that you can see on the screen can be selected with the mouse, and then copied from the application, a switch made back to HyperStudio, and the information pasted into you stack there. U.S. Atlas is a good example of where this procedure works very nicely. In addition, this can be used in any word processor to copy and paste text between the applications.

In describing this, we'll assume you have your HyperStudio stack already open.

1. Go to the application list under the icon at the far right of your menu bar, and choose Hide HyperStudio. This will temporarily hide your stack from view, and show you the desktop.

2. Launch your other application from you hard disk or CD-ROM drive.

3. Use the program to locate the text you are interested in, and highlight the passage using the mouse.

   NOTE: If you cannot highlight the text with the mouse, then this particular program does not support direct text copy-and-paste. See section D for work-around ideas for that situation.

4. Choose Copy from the Edit menu. This will place the information on the clipboard. (The clipboard is the name for the invisible place where information can be temporarily held after a Copy action. See your Macintosh manual for more information on the clipboard).

5. Now use the application list menu at the far right of the menu bar to switch back to HyperStudio.

6a. If the text object within which you wish to place you text already exists, click inside the text object at the position where you want your text to appear, and choose Paste Text from HyperStudio's Edit menu. The text will now appear within the text object.

6b. If a text object does not already exist into which you want to place your text, use Add a Text Object from the Objects menu to create one. Once sized and positioned, you can click within the text object, and choose Paste to place the text from the clipboard within the newly-created text object.

If you have multiple phrases of text which you wish to move, simply use the application list at the far right of the menu bar to move back and forth between the application and your HyperStudio stack. Continue the copy and paste process as needed.

When you are finished using the other program, move back to that program and Quit. You will then be returned to the Finder. Go back to the application list in the menu bar, and choose HyperStudio to resume your activities there.

B. Moving the Text Using the Clipboard - One Program Open

If your computer does not have enough memory to keep both HyperStudio and the other program open at the same time, you can use still use the clipboard as a temporary holding place for the information while you move back to HyperStudio to do your Paste.

1. With HyperStudio NOT open, run the information-resource application that you are interested in.

2. Use the features of your application program to locate the text passage, and highlight the section you wish to move.

3. Choose Copy from the Edit menu.

4. You can then close the first application, and open HyperStudio and load your stack.

5. Use the Move menu, if needed, to move back to the card that has the text object into which you wish to paste the information.

6. Then click the cursor within the text object at the position you wish the text to be placed, and choose Paste from the Edit menu. The text will now appear within the text object.

C. Moving the Text Using the Scrapbook

If you wish to collect numerous text passages in the first application before returning to HyperStudio, you can use the Scrapbook (found in the Apple menu) as a holding place for the information while you gather it.

1. With HyperStudio open or not, as your available memory allows, run the information-resource application that you are interested in.

2. Use the features of your application program to locate the text passage, and highlight the section you wish to move.

3. Choose Copy from the Edit menu.

4. Choose Scrapbook from the Apple menu, and then choose Paste from the Edit menu to place the information in the scrapbook. (The scrapbook will hold your information even when your computer has been turned off. See your Macintosh manual for more information.)

5. You can repeat steps 2-4 as many times as needed to gather all the information you wish.

6. You can then close the first application, and open HyperStudio and load your stack. Or, if you're keeping both open simultaneously, move back to HyperStudio through the applications list in the far right of the menu bar.

7. Use the Move menu, if needed, to move to the text object into which you wish to paste the information.

8. Open the Scrapbook, if necessary, and locate the piece of text you wish to paste into your HyperStudio stack. Use the scroll arrows in the Scrapbook to page through the saved data. Choose Copy from the Edit menu.

9. Then click the cursor within the text object at the position you wish the text to be placed and choose Paste from the Edit menu. The text will now appear within the text object.

10. Repeat steps 7-9 as needed to paste all the data.

11. To "clean up" the Scrapbook, use the scroll arrows to bring each piece of data into view, and then choose Cut to remove it from the Scrapbook. If you're not very error-prone, you can use Cut in step 8 to remove the data as you move it to your stack. However, if you "drop" the data by accidentally choosing Cut or Copy within HyperStudio, or on another "page" of the Scrapbook, whatever you were holding in the clipboard at that moment will be lost.

D. Save Text to a Disk or Hard Drive

Some programs, although they don't offer selectable text with Copy-and-Paste, will let you export text to a disk file. Grolier's is a good example of this type of program.

At this point we assume you have understood the options of either keeping both programs (your application and HyperStudio) open at the same time, or how to run one, and then the other to move between the two.

1. Starting in the program with the text data, use "Export Text", or "Save Selected Text", or a similar option (usually under the File menu) to save the text to disk. You may want to just save the files on the desktop to make them easier to locate later, but in any case, remember where you have saved the files.

If you are given any options about the format of the selected text, do NOT choose "individual lines of text" (this breaks up the paragraphs), or things like "Save as Word Document", that suggest that the text will be saved in a format specific to a particular word processing application. What you want is to just save the pure text, with as little additional embellishment as possible.

2. Save any other additional passages of text, as needed.

3. Quit the application program, and open your stack project in HyperStudio.

4. Move to the card in your stack where you wish to place the new information.

If you have not yet created the text object on that card, use Add a Text Object from the Objects menu to create one. While creating it...

5a. In the Text Appearance screen (before pressing "OK") choose Get a File.

5b. Choose "Desktop" (or wherever you placed your file) and locate your saved file.

5c. Open the saved file, and the text will appear within the text object that you have created.

Note: If your file does not appear in the file list when you use Get File, and you are sure you have saved it, it is probably not saved as a simple text file, and you may need to capture the text through a different method. See section D for "last resorts".

If you already have a text object on the card:

5a. Use the browse tool to click within the text object at the point that you want your text to appear.

5b. Choose Import Text from the File menu.

Where Text Is Inserted: If you click in the middle of a body of text within a text object in a HyperStudio stack, the imported text will be inserted at that point.

Remember to click at the beginning of the text object if that is where you want the next text to appear, or the middle or end as appropriate.

When the Menu Choices Change: The pair of entries in the File menu, Import Background/Save Screen, vs. Import Text/Export Text change according to whether you are using the paint tools, or have clicked in a text field. If you click in a text field with the browse tool, the menu choices change to Import Text/Export Text. If you choose a paint tool, or have not yet clicked in a text field with the browse tool, the choices will be Import Background/Save Screen.

If the text appears misaligned when it is brought into the text object in your stack, it is probably because of "return" characters at the end of each line. Use the mouse to select the unwanted space between portions of the text, and press the Delete key to eliminate them.

E: What To Do If There Is No Text Save, or Copy-Paste

Some programs, such as the Animals CD, have no way of exporting text at all. In these, you only have two alternatives:

a) Open up the Notepad desk accessory in the Apple menu, and position it on the screen while the other program is open, and manually type in the information. Once typed into the notepad, copy and paste can be used to move the text to HyperStudio. The reason for using the Notepad is just that it is easier to transcribe the text with the original in view.

b) Use the screen capture utility, PICTify, or the Shift-Command-3 option, described in the upcoming Graphics section, to turn the screen with the text on it into clip-art. The text will not be editable, but if what you are trying to do is just quickly get a phrase or paragraph that is already presented in a formatted text box or similar, this "last resort" approach may be all you need.

Graphics

Graphics are probably one of the easiest things to move between programs, because even in the worst case, if you can see it on the screen in your "other" program, you can always capture it right from the screen, save it to disk, and then bring it into your stack project with the Add Clip-Art, Load Background, or Add a Graphic menu choices.

For scanners, paint programs, and other cases where a total image is generated, the save to disk, and load from within HyperStudio is probably the best approach.

For reference programs, the best situation is for those programs that support the Copy and Paste menu items within them, so that the images can be easily moved from one program to another via the clipboard or scrapbook.

If you haven't read the "Text" section, please do so, as this section relies on the information provided there as a foundation. In addition to the methods described for text, there is the option of a direct screen capture.

A. Copying and Pasting Graphics

This approach is done in a manner very similar to text, at least as far as the capture process goes. In your other program, look to see if the Copy choice in the Edit menu is active (not grayed out). If it is available, choosing it may capture whatever graphic is on the screen at that moment. In a paint program, you may also be able to use a selector tool to specify just what part of the image you wish to copy to the clipboard.

When you're back in your HyperStudio stack, use Paste to put the graphic on the screen. At this point, it is just as though you've used the Add Clip-Art menu choice. You can position the graphic, and then drop it by clicking outside the selected area. It then becomes part of your background screen.

If you want to turn the selected area into a graphic object: Choose Add Graphic Object from the Objects menu while the graphic is still selected. You'll be prompted with a dialog box that says "Do you want to turn the selected part of the screen into a graphic object?" Click on "yes" if that is what you indeed want to do.

B. Exchanging Data Through Disk Files

If the program has its own clip-art files on disk, you can very likely load them into HyperStudio with Add Clip-Art, Import Background, or Add a Graphic Object.

If the program (such as a paint program or scanner utility) allows you save graphics to disk, it probably does so as PICT files.

In either case, HyperStudio accepts a wide variety of graphics formats, and can load PICT, TIFF, GIF, JPEG, EPS, MacPaint and other file types without difficulty. If you are presented with a choice of file format in the other application, PICT files are the best choice. In addition, if you can save them as 256-color images, rather than thousands or millions of colors, it will save a great deal of room on your disk, and also require less memory to initially load into your HyperStudio stack.

Assuming that you have a picture file on disk that you wish to load into HyperStudio, just use the usual menu choices of Add Clip-Art, etc. as you would for the HyperStudio art.

If a file that you know is on your disk does not appear in the file selection list of HyperStudio, then it is not a standard file format, and will require that you capture it directly from the screen of the other program. See the next section for information on that.

C. Taking a "Snapshot" of a Screen

(This is a method of capturing what is on the screen when you are unable to save it by other methods.)

The Macintosh has a built-in screen capture function. When you press Shift-Command-3, you'll hear a sound like that of a camera taking a picture, and a file named "Picture 1" (or 2, 3, etc.) will be saved in the main directory of your startup hard disk. This method captures the entire screen, including menu bars, etc. The good part is that it works in virtually every program without having to install any additional utility.

To capture a screen from almost any program:

1. Begin with the program running, and the image you are trying to "photograph" on the screen.

2. Press (and hold down) these keys in the following order - Shift, Command, 3. You will then hear a "snapshot" sound and a file will be created on your hard drive called "Picture 1". (Subsequent snapshots will be called "Picture 2", "Picture 3", etc... Once saved, you may rename them as you would any file.)

3. Close the program and open HyperStudio and move to the card on which you want to place a particular graphic image.

4. Under File choose Add Clip Art.

5. Within the file selection dialog, click the Desktop button, and then open your startup hard drive volume. In many cases, this is named "Macintosh HD".

6. Locate your newly created picture file and open it. It will be named Picture 1, etc. unless you renamed them from the Finder.

7. Use the Selector Tool to select the portion of the graphic you will need, and click on OK.

8. While the flashing dots are still present on the screen, use the mouse to position it where you wish, and then click outside the flashing dots to drop the graphic in place. While the dots are flashing, you can re-size the graphic if you wish.

9. If you wish to create a graphic object, you can choose Add a Graphic Object while the dots are still flashing.

Remember: "Clip-Art" is made part of the background, and can be edited with the paint tools. Graphic Objects float above the background, and can only be moved, re-sized or deleted with the arrow tool.

D. Using "PICTify" to Capture Selected Parts of a Screen - With Names!

"PICTIFY" is a program developed by Scott A. Johnson. It has been included in the HyperStudio package to allow you to capture just part of the screen in another program, and give that file a name as you save it.

PICTify is located in the HS Utilities folder, and is a Control Panel file that is installed by placing it in your System folder. Once installed, you can activate it by pressing a combination of the Shift, Control, Option and Command keys. You can configure the combination used to your own convenience.

Once installed, PICTify is used very much like the Shift-Command-3 approach, except that when you press the designated key combination, a crosshair cursor appears, which functions just like the rectangular selector tool in HyperStudio. Press the mouse button to start selecting the area you wish to capture, and drag to create the rectangle. When you release the mouse button, you'll be given a dialog box that allows you to name the file, and place it wherever you wish on your hard disk.

There is also an option for whether to save the file as a Pict or ResEdit file. Use the Pict file format for use with HyperStudio.

This utility is very elegant and useful. A big "thanks!" to Scott Johnson for making it available!

NOTE: When you use "Import a Background" to bring in a graphic that is smaller than your card, you'll get a question about whether to re-size the graphic to fit. If the graphic is a lot smaller than your card, the stretched graphic will probably not be very attractive. On the other hand, if the graphic is close in size, and you wanted it to be automatically sized, you can use that feature of HyperStudio to do the job!

Icons: A Special Case of Graphics

Icons are a special form of graphics used by programs. They are not PICT files, or any other type of simple clip-art, but actually include a group of elements that tell the computer what to do when the graphic is highlighted, etc.

There are several different types of icons, and currently HyperStudio can read the type called "xxxx". HyperStudio cannot read types "aaa", "bbb", and "ccc".

There are two ways to bring Icons into HyperStudio. The first is to just directly open Icon library files, such as the one included in the HS Art folder.

This is done by just clicking on the Disk Library option after choosing "Icons" in the Button Appearance dialog box.

Another, more obscure, source of icons is within other programs and documents. As an "Experienced User" (a checkbox in HyperStudio's Preferences dialog box), you can actually open other program and document files from within HyperStudio, and extract any icons of a readable type that may be present there.

For example, in HyperCard stacks you can find icons that could be used for your own buttons.

To access an icon embedded in a program or document, check the "Experienced User" box in the Preferences dialog box.

Then, when you create a button, click on Icons, and then Disk Library. When the file selection list appears, select a file that you think might have icons in it. If it doesn't, you'll get a message to that effect. However, if it does have icons, you'll see the scrolling list of them, just as you do with the usual set of HyperStudio icons.

Note that as an Experienced User, HyperStudio does not "filter", or hide, any of the files presented when you are looking for icons within other programs or documents. Just because a file is displayed, doesn't mean that you'll find any icons within it.

On the other hand, one place where you will very likely find other icons is in HyperStudio stacks! If you ever see a stack that has a nifty icon that you like in it for a given button and want to quickly access it, this is the way to do it! Just choose the HyperStudio stack from within the file list of the Icon Disk Library feature!

Sound

Sounds are different from text and graphics, in that they can't be copied and pasted from another application to HyperStudio.

However, they may exist on the other program's disk as stand-alone files, or be able to be saved as individual files by that program. In addition, just as with icons, as an "Experienced User" (a checkbox in HyperStudio's Preferences dialog box), you can actually open other program and document files from within HyperStudio, and extract them to use in your own stacks!

A. Adding Sounds From Disk Files (Disk or CD-ROM)

This is the most likely way that you will get sounds into a stack that you are creating. If the sounds from the other resource program are files on a disk, chances are very good that HyperStudio can read them. HyperStudio reads AIFF, AIFC, Sound Resource files, Apple IIGS sound files, and even PC-compatible ".WAV" files!

1. While creating a button in your HyperStudio stack, choose "Play a Sound".

2. In the Tape Deck screen, choose "Disk Library".

4. Next click on "Desktop", and from there find your sound file and open it.

5. Your file should now be named on the Tape Deck screen. You may rename it and play it at this point.

6. Click "OK" when done.

B. Accessing an "Embedded" Sound

If the sound is not a stand-alone file, it may still be possible to "find" it within a program or document.

To access a sound embedded in a program or document, check the "Experienced User" box in the Preferences dialog box.

Then, when you create a button, click on Play a Sound in the Button Actions dialog, and then Disk Library. When the file selection list appears, select a file that you think might have sounds in it. If it doesn't, you'll get a message to that effect. However, if it does have sounds, you'll see the scrolling list of them, just as you do with the usual set of HyperStudio sample sounds. For many programs, it's not easy to tell which files have sounds, and it's just a matter of hunting through files for sounds that you can find, or "know" that are there.

Note that as an Experienced User, HyperStudio does not "filter", or hide, any of the files presented when you are looking for sounds within other programs or documents. Just because a file is displayed, doesn't mean that you'll find any sounds within it.

On the other hand, as with icons, one place where you will very likely find other sounds is in HyperStudio stacks! If you ever see a stack that has a sound in it that you like, and want to quickly access it, this is the way to do it! Just choose the HyperStudio stack from within the file list of the Play a Sound Disk Library feature!

QuickTime Movies

There are several different ways of storing digital movies within programs, but QuickTime movies are certainly the most common, and considered the standard for the Macintosh.

QuickTime movies, and portions thereof can be copied and pasted between applications that support this feature (HyperStudio does), however, direct file access is the easiest approach.

When you choose "Play a QuickTime Movie" in the Actions dialogs of HyperStudio, you can explore a CD-ROM disk just as you would a folder on your hard disk. Any QuickTime movies will be listed in the file selection window, often with a "Preview" frame that will give you an idea of what that movie that file contains.

Not all CD-ROM titles use meaningful file names, however. You may find files just labeled Movie1, Movie2, etc. In the case of the Grolier's and Animals CD-ROMs, the sections on those programs in this manual contain an indexed list of those files, and their actual contents. It is likely that future editions of many CD-ROM titles will have more clearly labeled movie files as more people begin to use them as resources, rather than just onetime entertainment events.

Shortcuts and Tips (READ!!!! READ!!!! READ!!!!)

Using your toolbox after placing a QuickTime Movie onto the card will often knock the movie off of the card! Therefore use any toolbox items prior to adding your QuickTime movie.

Since your text is often the most easily adjusted portion of a card, it is often best to add a text box last.

Re-sizing the movie may cause it to play more slowly. You may want to leave it the size it is when it first appears.

Unless you have stored your movie on your hard drive, HyperStudio will expect to find the CD-ROM where the movie is stored inside the computer during play. If it is not loaded in the computer when that card comes up, the program will ask you to load the source of the movie.

A Word About Copyrights

In the use of all of these data forms, there is the issue of what you can use in your own projects, and whether you can share the resulting projects with others.

Although an entire book could undoubtedly be written on this subject, as with most things, there is a simple answer.

All commercial sources of information come with some sort of a license agreement that defines what you can and can't do with that material. Generally speaking, for your own entertainment, and within the bounds of your own personal use, you can use the images any way you want. Of course, careful reading may reveal phrases like "the contents of this may not be altered in any way". Not even counting sharing with others, that pretty much limits your options right there, technically speaking.

On the other hand, there is also a growing list of what we call "Copyright Friendly" resources, that are meant to be used in multimedia projects, and shared with others as well! Rather than stress yourself out over the companies that limit the use of their product, we recommend you energetically support those that encourage the creative use of their resources.

For example, all of the resources in the HyperStudio package can be used in your own projects, which can in turn be shared with others, without limitation, other than our asking that you not sell the clip-art, etc. for its own intrinsic value. That is, you can't take the HyperStudio resources and repackage them to sell as "Joe's Great Clip-Art".

Not all of the packages described in this Appendix are "copyright friendly", but they are listed because they are some of the more frequently found programs that you may have questions about.

In all your projects, using the HyperStudio Bibliography template (in Ready Made Cards), is a good way to let others know where the resources within your projects have come from.

Program Directory

In the following pages are brief descriptions of various programs, and particular notes about how to use data from them within your own HyperStudio projects.

As an additional aid, the following letters are used so that you can quickly tell which data types are accessible in a particular program:

Key:

T - Text will transfer.

G - Graphics will transfer.

S - Sound will transfer.

Q - QuickTime movies will transfer.

The Programs...

The Print Shop (T, G)

To save graphics in The Print Shop take a snapshot of the screen. Text is treated as a graphic in The Print Shop and cannot be moved separately.

Shortcuts and Tips

Print Shop graphics are small, and re-sizing them to use as a background won't give very good results. However, you'll find them useful as bits of clip-art on a card.

While creating in The Print Shop, you may want to decide beforehand whether your graphic would be best developed as a vertical or horizontal graphic, thereby lessening distortion in the transfer.

Kid Pix (G, S, Q)

Text

Text is treated as a graphic in Kid Pix and cannot be moved separately.

Graphics

Graphics can be chosen from within HyperStudio.

Sound

Kid Pix allows the user to attach a sound file to created graphics. That sound will not automatically transfer when the graphic is moved to HyperStudio. To transfer the sound to HyperStudio, use the tapedeck to add the sound from a stand-alone file found in the Kid Pix folder.

Note: If you would like your sound to play automatically, create a magic button while in the "Add a Button" mode.

Kid Pix QuickTime Video:

Kid Pix QuickTime Videos are accessible from within HyperStudio.

1. In your HyperStudio stack, go to "Objects" and create a button to play a "Movie or Video".
2. Next choose "QuickTime Movie".
3. Click on "Desktop" in the file selection dialog box, and choose the "Quick Picks" folder in Kid Pix.
4. Select a movie and open it. The first frame of the movie will appear on your card with the flashing dots around it. Position it on your card.
6. Next you will see your preview screen. You may click on "Try It" to see the

movie run or reposition at this point. You can also get another movie at this point. Click "OK" when done.

Note: QuickTime movies are not embedded in your HyperStudio stacks. Rather, a "pointer" is just kept to where to find the movie. This means that the Kid Pix folder must be available with the movies when you click on the button in your HyperStudio stack.

If you want to move your stack to another disk, or play the movies without requiring the Kid Pix folders, use the Finder to make a copy of the movie file, and move it to the same folder as your stack.

Kid Pix Slide Show

If you have the "Slide Show" program with your Kid Pix application, you can easily transfer the slide show to "HyperStudio" by saving the slide show as a QuickTime Movie and importing it in the following manner:

1. In your HyperStudio stack, go to "Objects" and create a button to play a "Movie or Video".

2. Next choose "QuickTime Movie".

3. Choose "Desktop" and click on your slide show.

4. Open it. The first frame of the movie will appear on your card and will be ready for use. Sound will automatically transfer.

The Writing Center (T, G)

Text

1. To move text from The Writing Center, you will have to use the clipboard or scrapbook.

Note: Although The Writing Center allows the user to create columns of text, the text will not transfer into the HyperStudio text box in columns. If you wish to import the text in the column format, it is probably best to take a "snapshot". However, your snapshot will be limited to the amount of text you can see on your screen at one time.

Graphics

1. In HyperStudio, go to your card.

2. Under "File" choose "Import Background".

3. Choose "Desktop" and locate the folder named "pictures - wrtg.ctr".

4. Open it to see the many files of graphics. Select the graphic you want by double-clicking.

5. Allow HyperStudio to re-size the graphic if it is to be a background. ("Add Clip Art" is also a function which will work with these graphics.)

Grolier's Multimedia Encyclopedia (T, G, Q)

Text

Text from Grolier's can be saved within Grolier's as a regular text file to a disk or to the hard drive. It cannot be copied or pasted.

Graphics

1. Since graphics cannot be saved in the Grolier's program, you will need to take a "snapshot" of the screen and move it to HyperStudio as clip art.

2. In Version 7 of Grolier's, there are a number of picture files on disk, some of which are quite useful. Although no organized index is available, some of the file names are meaningful enough that you can find some interesting things.

Within the "Z0, Z1, etc." folders of the Grolier's version 7 CD, files that end in ".PCT" are program image files, and not of any particular use. On the other hand, files that end in ".PIH" are usable graphics.

Sound

Although version 6 of Grolier's has sound embedded in the application, it is not accessible through HyperStudio. Version 7, on the other hand, has a number of sound files. These are found in the "pix" folder, and also as sound-only QuickTime movie files.

QuickTime Movies

You can import QuickTime Movies from Grolier's.

Not all QuickTime movies in Grolier's have sound, and not all of them have pictures! In version 7, the files that have the form "snd103.mov" are QuickTime "sound" files. That is, there is only a sound track, and no accompanying video. This can still be played by a HyperStudio button as a QuickTime movie, with the end result being the playing of the desired sound.

U.S. Atlas (T,G,S)

Text

Can be put on a clipboard or scrapbook.

Graphics

In U.S. Atlas there is a "Save" feature for graphics. Note that the topmost layer of the screen is saved. For example, if you pull up a map and then open the flag graphic, the flag will be saved.

1. In U.S. Atlas save the image you want to a disk or the hard drive.

Note: You may want to rename the saved graphic as all graphics saved will automatically be named "Untitled PICT".

2. Open HyperStudio and go to the card you need. Under "File" choose "Load Background" or "Add Clip Art".

Note: If you want to be sure that your map will cover the entire card, it is best to load it as clip art.

3. Choose "Desktop" and find the file you created.

4. Open it and add it to your card.

Sound

Sound files may be added from U.S. Atlas as stand-alone sound files using the tapedeck in HyperStudio.

Shortcuts and Tips:

There are state anthems on U.S. Atlas in files which are numbered 1-50. These correspond to the alphabetical list of all the states.

World Atlas (T, G, S, Q)

Text

See U.S. Atlas.

Graphics

See U.S. Atlas. Note that there are graphs in World Atlas.

Sound

See U.S. Atlas. There are country anthems, but they are not as clearly numbered as those in U.S. Atlas. You will find them in folder Af. Folder Sf contains country names as sound.

QuickTime Movies

Folder Vf contains the QuickTime Movies and they are labeled with country names.

The Animals (T, G, Q)

Text

Must be transferred via the clipboard.

Graphics

Must be captured from the screen.

QuickTime Movies

Look in the "Media" folder for "Movies". However, these movies are numbered and there are no clues in the numeration.

Mammals (G,S,Q)

Graphics

Must be captured from the screen.

Sound

Can be added directly from the HyperStudio tapedeck as stand-alone files. There are several files which will speak single words. In the "Mammals Annex" the file "Animals" will say animal names and they are clearly labeled. "Subspecies" and "Orders" are also clearly labeled and are spoken, single-word sounds.

QuickTime Movies

Note that these movies have no sound. They are located in the "Movie" folder.

ClarisWorks (T,G)

Text

1. Begin inside ClarisWorks with your text on the screen before you.

2. From the "File" menu, choose "Save As".

3. In the available format box in the lower left of the screen, you will see the word ClarisWorks. This is a pull-down menu. Pull it down and select "Text".

4. Then choose "Save". This will save your text as a text file instead of a ClarisWorks file, which HyperStudio will not read.

5. Next go into your HyperStudio card.

6. Under "Objects", choose "Add a Text Item".

7. After creating your text style and BEFORE pressing "O.K.", choose "Get File".

8. Choose "Desktop" and find your file and open it.

9. Your ClarisWorks text will now appear in the text window of HyperStudio.

Graphics:

1. Begin inside ClarisWorks with your graphic on the screen before you.

2. Choose "Save As" from the File menu.

3. In the available format box in the lower left of the screen, you will see the

word ClarisWorks. This is a pull-down screen. Pull it down and select "PICT". Then choose "Save".

4. Now open your HyperStudio card.

5. Under "File" choose "Add Clip Art".

6. Choose "Desktop".

7. Find your file and open it.

8. You will be presented with the usual clip-art choices and can now add your ClarisWorks graphic to your HyperStudio card.

Shortcuts and Tips

ClarisWorks documents can be launched from a HyperStudio button by using the Connect to Another Program button action. You can add a button which connects your card directly to a specific ClarisWorks document, or the application in general. (See "Adding a Button".) HyperStudio will then launch the ClarisWorks file directly. This is helpful when making presentations in which the text or information changes regularly, or you wish to demonstrate the features of a program such as ClarisWorks.

HyperCard (G)

Text

Some text fields in HyperCard stacks are read-only, and as such can only be captured as a screen graphic. (See section II.B). On the other hand, editable text fields can be accessed by selecting text and using Copy & Paste.

Graphics

While editing a HyperCard stack, you can use the selector tool of the paint tools to select, copy and paste graphics. You can also export screens as graphics. For HyperCard "application" stacks that are not accessible through the menus, you can always take a "snapshot" of the screen with Shift-Command-3, or PICTify.

Sounds

HyperCard stacks can be opened when HyperStudio's Preferences are set to "Experienced User". From there, you'll see a list of sounds in a particular stack, which can then be extracted.

Shortcuts and Tips:

HyperCard stacks can be launched from a HyperStudio button by using the Connect to Another Program button action. You can add a button which connects your card directly to a specific HyperCard document, or the application in general. (See "Adding a Button".) HyperStudio will then launch the HyperCard file directly. This is helpful when making presentations in which the text or information changes regularly, or you wish to demonstrate the features of a program such as HyperCard.

Encarta (T,G,S)

Text

Text can be copied to the clipboard.

Graphics

Must be accessed by taking a snapshot.

Sound

Sounds from Encarta are stored in the program application file.

QuickTime

QuickTime movies are in the Encarta folder.

Summary

Remember, there are only four basic data types to be shared between programs: text, sounds, graphics and digital movies. We hope that the discussion and examples here have given you a good start on using the data in many different programs.

Now that you are familiar with the different ways to incorporate the resources from other programs into HyperStudio, try experimenting with some of your other favorites!

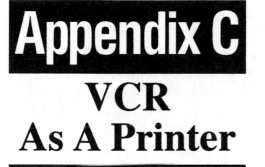

Appendix C
VCR
As A Printer

This appendix is designed to help you explore the exciting new idea of using your TV/monitor for computer-based presentations, and using the VCR as a "printer" for the computer.

Once your system is set up, you'll be able to record presentations! Here are a few suggested uses and ideas:

If you are a teacher, using the VCR as a printer in the classroom can open up some great opportunities! For example:

- Send student presentations home to parents
- Record class projects and share them with other teachers and administrators;
- Create training tapes for other staff members in your school or district;
- Create "portfolios" of projects to take to conferences and other meetings to share what you've been doing with computers–without having to take any more equipment than a single videotape!

Reference

This is the minimum setup you'll need to record computer presentations on a video cassette recorder (VCR). It provides for the **video signal** to be sent from the computer to the TV/monitor; and, provides for the **audio signal** to be sent from both the computer and a microphone.

Descriptions:

TV: This is any standard television or monitor. It's used for viewing the video output.

VCR: The video cassette recorder is used to capture both the audio and video signals.

Audio Mixer: The audio mixer receives audio signals from various sources—such as the computer and a microphone—and sends out a single audio signal. This is necessary since the VCR usually has only one audio input. The Multimedia Sound Recording Kit, from Roger Wagner Publishing, provides both the sound mixer and all necessary cables to make the proper connections.

NTSC Converter: This converts the computer video signals to signals the VCR can understand and use. Two products which accomplish this are the Presenter's Plus™ and TelevEyes Pro™, both available from Roger Wagner Publishing. If your Macintosh is the "AV" type, you won't need either of these.

Computer: This is any standard Macintosh computer. For the audio output, use a mini-phono adaptor (Radio Shack part #274-387) or the appropriate cable from the RWP Sound Recording Kit.

Minimum VCR/Computer Setup

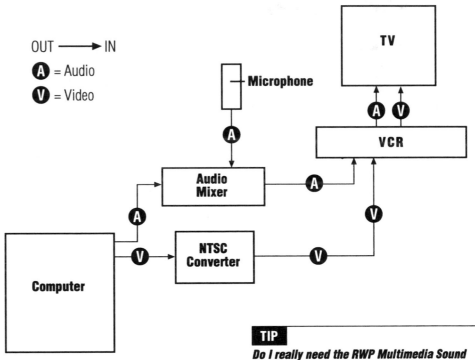

TIP

Do I really need the RWP Multimedia Sound Recording Kit?

This is a must if you intend to record more than just the computer sounds, such as student narration or any other external sound source. As an added bonus, the Sound Recording Kit comes complete with all the cables and adaptors you'll need.

This setup provides for **recording** presentations (both video and audio portions), and for **digitizing** images from various video sources. A video source can be any kind of equipment that produces a video signal. In this diagram we show a laserdisc player, video camera and a second VCR as sources for digitizing images on the computer.

TIP

What does the Audio/Visual Selector do?

The "Audio/Visual Selector" provides a way to switch from one **video source** and **audio source** to another. It has two groups of buttons on the front of the unit which allow a variety of choices:

The left group of buttons let you choose which video image you see on the TV, which is also the image the VCR is recording. You can view and record the image coming from your computer, laserdisc player, video camera or a second VCR.

The right group of buttons let you choose which image you will see on the computer screen for digitizing video images for use as clip art. You can select images coming from your computer, laserdisc player, video camera or a second VCR.

For a detailed diagram on how to connect the wires, refer to the illustration on the next page.

Wiring Setup

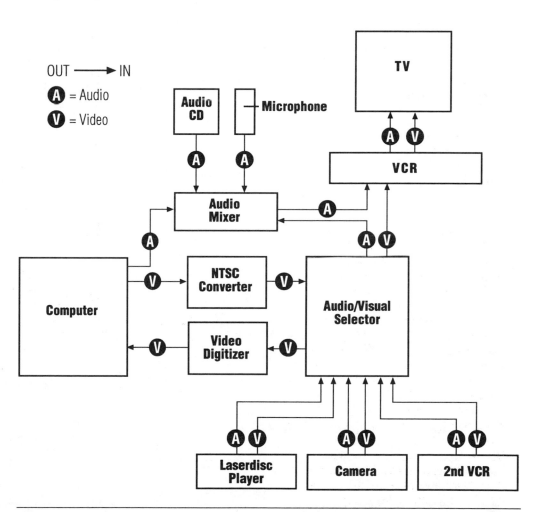

The underlying principles to this whole process are very simple: There are two signals (or to be more direct, "flavors" of wires) you'll need to be aware of. One is the *video signal,* which carries the picture from the computer to the VCR, and from there to a classroom TV or monitor. The other is the *audio signal,* which carries the sound from the computer to the VCR, and on to the TV or monitor. The Multimedia Sound Recording Kit and the Radio Shack Audio/Visual Selector simply work as "traffic cops" to route the signals through their proper channels.

TIPS

What is an "RF Modulator"?

Many video devices, such as camcorders, laserdisc players, and others, send out video signals which cannot be "picked up" by TV's. An RF Modulator changes these video signals to a standard TV signal. If your TV/Monitor has "video in" and "audio in" composite inputs, you'll not need an RF Modulator.

What is a "Mini-phono adapter"?

This is a small connector which plugs into the computer headphone jack (sound out on the CPU) to the RWP Multimedia Sound Recording Kit. Most Macintosh computers use the same kind of "connector" you see on the mini-headphones that are used with many small tape players.

Wiring Detail

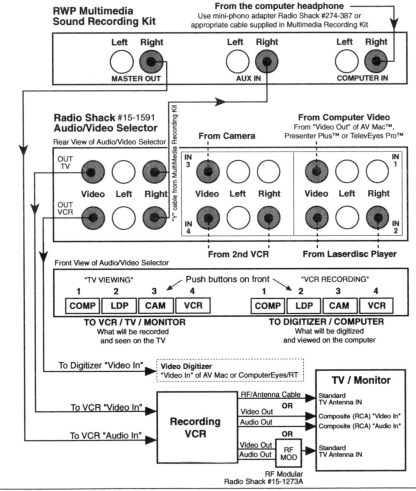

Appendix D
Memory
&
Disk Use

Memory & Disk Use

HyperStudio and your stacks use both memory and disk space. Understanding how and when each is used will help you get the best performance out of your system, especially as your projects become more complex.

The good news is that HyperStudio manages both disk and memory use to a large extent, so that in the usual course of events, you don't have to know anything about the inner workings. However, as with most things, a good understanding of what is actually going on in your computer will let you extend your use beyond what can be found in any manual.

Disk Use

When a stack is saved on to your disk, it is as one specific file. In general, since a high density 3.5" disk holds 1.4mb, you would not want to create stacks that are greater than about 1.3mb (there's always a little "overhead" for the disk file structure).

As you create your stack, any sounds, graphics, text objects, etc. that you create are all part of the stack file. The only exception to this are QuickTime movies.

QuickTime Movies: When you create a button or other element that activates a QuickTime movie, what is actually contained in your stack is a *pointer* to the movie file, wherever it happens to be located. For this reason, it is important, when you move a stack to another location, make sure that the movie file will still be available ("online"). If this is not possible, then move the movie file itself to the same folder as the stack, so that the stack will be able to find the movie when the time comes.

QuickTime movies approximately 100k per second that the movie plays. This is approximate, and can vary depending on a number of factors, most notably what kind of compression was used when the movie was created. However, this general guideline is easy to remember, and lets you keep in mind that you could put about 14 seconds of video on a single disk. This is "not much" on the one hand, but then again, it is quite possible to clearly illustrate a concept or process in just 3-4 seconds. This means you can easily create a small project on a single floppy disk that discusses a subject, and also includes an individual QuickTime movie to demonstrate a particular idea along the way.

A common misconception is that QuickTime movies require large amounts of memory. What they do require is disk space. The HyperStudio System CD includes a QuickTime movies that is over 50mb in size, and yet very few computers have this much RAM. It should be obvious that movies are "rolled through" memory, and are not necessarily loaded in their entirety. The only exception would be very short movies, where in fact, if there is enough memory, the entire movie is kept in memory while it is being used. However, in the end, all this is transparent to the user, so is of little concern.

Sounds, when recorded in HyperStudio, are also written to disk, even while your stack is still in memory. HyperStudio compresses the sounds you record by a factor of 6:1. The net result is that each second of sound will take up about 4k of memory on disk. When a sound is played, the entire sound is loaded into memory, but the memory is then made available again after the sound has completed. What this means is that you can have virtually as many different sound files as you like, as long as there is sufficient free memory (see the upcoming section on that) to load the particular sound file at that moment.

Text requires 1 byte of disk space per character, and as such is virtually "free", when considered in the context of the size of typical disk storage. A printed page, for example, holds about 3,000 characters (3k). Thus a 1.4mb disk could hold over 450 pages. Like we said, it's basically "free"!

In the end, it is the graphic data that occupies the largest portion of your disk file. Graphics that are imported into HyperStudio arc automatically optimized and compressed. The biggest variable is whether your stack is set to 16 or 256 colors. For general planning purposes, figure that every card will take 25k at 16 colors, and 50k at 256 colors. This is independent of the source of the graphic. It doesn't matter whether the file was originally a photograph or clip-art, or a PICT or TIFF formatted file. Once loaded into your stack, HyperStudio uses the same storage system for all graphics.

Photographs DO take more disk storage than clip-art in general, but it isn't the source of the image that is the cause, but rather the pattern of the image (or more accurately, lack of a pattern) that results in the higher disk storage requirements.

When a graphic is compressed, HyperStudio looks for areas of solid color. Wherever that can be found, the picture can be more effectively compressed when stored to disk. For example, an entire card background, but of one solid color, can be stored in as little as 2k of disk space.

However, as lines appear on the screen, the computer can't take advantage of as much "solid color space", and more disk space is required. One of HyperStudio's simple map graphics, such as the "USA" map, for example, requires about 29k (at 256 colors). Photographs take more disk space because there are no extensive areas of just one solid color.

A photograph that fills an entire card will take about 75-100k of disk space. Of course, keep in mind that a given card is actually usually a combination of solid colors and other graphics, so a quarter screen photograph might use 25k, and the remainder of the card could take quite little additional space.

In general, you can estimate that every card in a 256-color stack will take 50k of disk space, even including sounds, your text, and other elements. This can obviously vary, but it's an easy number to remember, and let's you easily estimate (for example) that an 1.4mb disk could hold 28 cards (at 256 colors).

This is a good time to mention by the way, that the same disk could hold *56 cards* if it were a 16 color stack. Although many people instinctively choose the higher color level, it isn't always necessary for a given project. It's also possible to connect different stacks together, and the stacks can individually be a different color levels. When you are planning your projects, the most important thing is to start with your communication objective, then look at how much space you have available to hold that message, and then plan your elements accordingly. Even at 16 colors, HyperStudio can display photographs that are still quite recognizable.

Finally, stacks can also be connected from one disk to another. If your project consists of more stacks than can fit on a single floppy disk, just make the "connect to another stack" action point to the stack on the "next" disk. This is done by just choosing the "connect to another stack" action, and then while the file selection dialog is open, ejecting the current floppy, inserting the next one, and choosing the next stack in the series. After the connection is made, HyperStudio will automatically prompt you to switch the floppies back when you choose "Save" from the file menu, or at any other time that the original disk is required to be back in the drive.

When the stack series if finally run, HyperStudio will also automatically prompt for the correct floppy disk to be inserted as necessary.

Memory

We started with the discussion of disk storage, because in the end, everything that is held in memory, on either a long- or short-term basis, has to be stored on the disk. If you know the disk space required by the different elements, then you also already understand how memory is used, because the amounts are pretty much equivalent.

When a stack is opened, the entire series of card backgrounds is brought into memory, along with any graphic objects, text objects and buttons. However, some elements are left on disk until they are needed. This conserves memory, and lets you play "larger" stacks than would otherwise fit in memory. Notice that HyperStudio uses a mixed approach to memory use. That is, the entire stack's series of cards is loaded into memory, but certain elements are kept on disk. The particular approach that HyperStudio uses gives an optimum performance of your final project.

By contrast, some multimedia systems keep everything on disk until needed. Although this lets them boast "one file systems", the file itself can grow *very* large on disk, and ultimately make it impossible to use floppy disks, but it also tends to make every action in your stack seem sluggish as the system must constantly go to the disk to get the next element that is displayed.

With HyperStudio stacks, everything is brought into memory when the stack is opened, except for QuickTime movies, sounds, icons and New Button Actions. These elements are loaded only when used, and also then immediately released to make room for other activities.

To find out how much memory is actually used by your stack, and how much additional information is on disk, you can choose "About this stack" from the Objects menu. There you'll see "Current memory used". This tells you how much memory the backgrounds, graphics, text items, etc. are currently using.

The next item, "Disk space needed" tells you what the total space required for your stack on disk is. The difference in the two numbers tells you how much disk space is used for your sounds, icons, etc.

The item directly below those two, "Available memory" tells you how much memory remains for additional elements and operations.

> **IMPORTANT**: The "Available memory" is not just how much memory remains in your entire computer, but rather, how much memory remains of the *partition of memory* that HyperStudio was allocated based on the number assigned through the Finder.

For example, at the time of the writing of this manual the HyperStudio application is

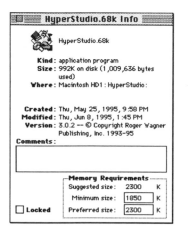

▲▲▲

Use the **Get Info** dialog in the **Finder** to increase available memory to HyperStudio.

set to a maximum partition size of 2300k (2.3mb). The HyperStudio application itself takes about 800k of memory to run, leaving approximately 1500k available, *regardless* of the total memory of your computer.

Memory Managing Ideas

Here are a few space saving and memory management ideas. If you are running into memory problems, try these out:

Increasing Available Memory

You can allocate more memory to HyperStudio from within the Finder with these simple steps:

1. Quit HyperStudio

2. Locate the HyperStudio application icon using the Finder.

3. Choose "Get Info" from the Finder's File menu (or press command-I).

4. Use the Info dialog to enter the amount of memory you want to allocate to HyperStudio.

5. Close the Info dialog and restart HyperStudio.

Keep in mind that HyperStudio, like all other applications, cannot use more memory than your computer has!

Segmenting Projects

Another approach to managing memory and stack size is "Stack Segmenting". This simply means keeping your entire project in smaller sized stacks, as opposed to one giant stack.

Just as this manual is broken up into small segments called *Chapters*, you can create your projects using the same approach. For example, if you were creating a project on your pets, you could have one stack called "My Dogs", the other "My Cats", and a third stack called "My Pets" (My Pets would act as a menu, or launcher, to the other two stacks). This not only helps keep your stacks smaller, but makes it more efficient if you wanted to, for example, add "My Birds" at a later date.

Disk Based Media

Also keep in mind that text, graphics, and sounds, can be made "disk-based" as opposed to keeping these materials in the stack itself. Using the disk based approach is totally optional.

Appendix E
Trouble Shooting

This appendix will get you started solving a problem you might encounter while using HyperStudio. If you can't find the solution here, be sure to check out the HyperStudio Tutorial as well!

If You Encounter a Problem...

HyperStudio has been carefully designed and tested to be an extremely reliable creative environment. In the end, "It's just supposed to work!" However, this section anticipates problems you may encounter where additional information about a necessary procedure, or particular explanation of an error message may be of help.

Additional tips are listed in the HyperStudio Tutorial.

If you do have a problem that cannot be resolved with the information here, please feel free to call our technical support department at 619-442-0522, Extension 13. Their hours of operation are Monday through Friday, 9:30 - 5:30 pm, Pacific Standard Time.

If you do call, please have the following information ready:

- Your HyperStudio serial number. This is displayed on the startup screen when you first run HyperStudio.
- The model of your Macintosh computer (Mac LC, or Quadra 660AV, for example).
- The version of your system software, for example, "system 7.5". This is found by using "About this Macintosh" from the Apple menu of the Finder (the desktop).
- A clear description of your problem. For example, the question "How can I make imported images sharper?" is much easier to be of help with than "When I try to use pictures, they don't work."

Before You Call... (Or, How to Be Your Own Technical Support)

Although we will be happy to help you through any difficulty you might encounter, you can save yourself time and trouble by using some of the same techniques professionals use, and also possibly avoid the need to call at all!

Before calling, try the "process of elimination" approach. If, for example, HyperStudio locked up when you try to add a picture, try some quick "comparisons" to see if you can identify the source of the problem. You might, for example:

a) Try the same procedure on another computer. If it works there, then the problem might be an unusual control panel or initialization file in your system folder of the problematic computer.

b) Start up the computer with the shift key down. This turns off all extensions in your system. If the problem goes away, then you know that it is an extension, not HyperStudio itself. If you do suspect an init or control panel problem, look in your Control Panels or Extensions folders for unusual add-ons, and move them to a temporary folder on your desktop. Those extensions that make your cursor look like a ray-gun can be cute, but they can also create problems!

c) Try performing a similar function in another program, for example, loading the same picture in ClarisWorks or a paint program. If it doesn't work there, then that's a clue that the file is not a picture file, or that it is VERY unusual, and requires some sort of conversion utility. (Note: in the case of graphics, HyperStudio does load more different kinds of files than most other programs of any kind).

d) If you were using a peripheral device such as a laserdisc player or CD-ROM drive, try the device with another software title that works with that device, if possible. Also, try the device with HyperStudio on another computer.

In general, the approach used in almost all trouble-shooting procedures is to compare how something behaves in one setting, versus how it does in another setting where only one suspected cause of the problem has been changed. One thing you should try to avoid is changing too many things at once. For example, if you try something on one computer, but then try a completely different picture file on another computer with a different application, and "it works", you won't know whether it which of the three variables was really the "clue" as to your problem!

On the following pages are specific questions or situations that we've anticipated. Keep the preceding tips in mind when tracking down solutions, check out the suggestions offered, and as always, give us a call if further help is needed!

"I'm importing images, and they don't look as nice as I'd like. Can the quality be improved?"

HyperStudio supports a number of different levels of colors for stacks. 16 color stacks take the least amount of memory, but digitized photos and QuickTime movies look noticeably grainy. A 256 color stack will display digitized photos and movies with greater clarity.

The first thing to check when importing a digitized image as clip-art is that your color menu has "lots" of colors (256), rather than 16. The color level of stacks can be set to 256 colors by choosing Stack Info from the Objects menu. Then click on the Change # of Colors or Card Size button. Then choose "lots of colors (256)" and click on OK.

If you start a new stack from the Home Stack, your new stack will automatically be set to 16 colors. If you want to change this "default", use The Change # of Colors just described to change your Home Stack to 256 colors, and then use Save from the File menu to just save it right back to the disk. Now any new stacks will start at 256 colors. If you are an "experienced HyperStudio user", you'll be asked the color level and card size whenever you start a new stack.

"Is there a way to get even better images?"

HyperStudio has some of the best image handling available in any program. In addition, it even supports "custom palettes". Imagine that you had a picture of a sunset that you wanted to use as a full-screen image for a given card. There would likely be many, many shades of red and orange in your image; many more shades than were normally provided in the standard color palette. Although Add Clip-Art will do a satisfactory job in loading the image as a part of a screen, HyperStudio is "clever" enough to do a little bit extra when you load the image as an entire screen - it will create a custom palette of the many more reds and oranges needed to make that particular picture look its best.

The general rule is simple: "Add Clip-Art" imports an image using whatever color palette is already used on the card. This is usually the standard palette. "Load Background" brings in the image and the special colors for the image (if available). The net result is that you can actually get images in HyperStudio's 256 colors that are almost indistinguishable from a thousands of colors image!

"When I load a stack, I get a message saying that only part of the stack could be loaded. What should I do?"

Although in theory, you should never get this message, in the real world, things do happen to files. Perhaps it's a mechanical problem with a disk drive, or a bit of someone's peanut butter sandwich that's found its way into a floppy disk. Regardless, when it happens, most programs would just tell you "Sorry, there was an error with your file, and you're not getting any of it back." With HyperStudio, the program will take some extra time to scan the disk, and attempt to recover as much of the file as possible. In most cases, it will succeed to at least some degree, and will change the "in-memory" name of your stack to include the suffix "(partial)", such as in "History of the World (partial)". This is so that you are alerted to the fact that you are working with a partial version of your project.

In any cases of an error like this, you should IMMEDIATELY use "Save As" from the File menu to save your stack as a fresh file to your hard disk, or a new floppy disk. You may also occasionally see a message saying that the "resource fork" of your file was damaged. With resource fork errors, the part of your stack that is lost is not the cards themselves, but any sounds that were added, and also any New Button Actions. In this case, you'll want to go back through your stack and edit the buttons that use sound effects, icons or New Button Actions, and re-add these as needed. One item of good news here: if a sound, icon or NBA is used for several buttons, re-adding it to one button will make it automatically reappear for all the other buttons that use that same sound or NBA!

How to minimize or diagnose floppy disk problems: 3.5" disk drives are not quite as reliable as hard disks, in part because of the media, and also because disks are often moved between many different computers and disk drives. If you do have problems, check the following things:

- Try to limit the number of computers that a given floppy is used on. Problems occur most often when moving from one computer to another.

- How old is the disk? Disks don't last forever. Occasionally used disks can last for years, but if the disk is used daily, it should not be used for more than a year or two.

- Note where problems occur. If you have a group of computers, make a note of which computer was involved when the error occurred, and also, if possible, the computer just before. What seems to be a random problem may be traceable to a particular computer. Remember that sometimes it's not the computer where the problem occurred, but the one before that the actually caused the problem.

"I can't seem to get my laserdisc player to work with HyperStudio. Is there something I need to check?"

This is one of those cases where "not working" can mean a variety of things. Depending on just which problem you're having, you'll need to check different possible causes.

The two main categories here are:

1. The computer communicating with the laserdisc player, telling it what image or motion sequence to display. Problems here show up with the HyperStudio dialog

box saying, "I can't find the laserdisc player". However, if you use a remote control for the laserdisc, or manually operate the buttons on the player, you should still be able to see the images on a TV-style monitor attached to the player.

2. The display of the image. Problems here show up as not being able to see the image, even though HyperStudio itself doesn't report any problems. This situation is simply a case of asking yourself how the video image is getting to the TV-style monitor on which the image should be displayed. There is a slight variation on this theme for "AV" Macs and PowerMacs.

We'll consider the two categories individually. First, situations that involve how the computer tells the laserdisc player what image to display. This is communicated to the player via a serial connecting cable (usually called a "CC04"), which is attached to the modem port of the computer. If you get the HyperStudio dialog box telling you it couldn't find the player, check the following:

- The kind of laserdisc player you are using. If you have a Sony laserdisc player, you will need to contact the HyperStudio Network at 609-466-3196 to order the Sony driver. Your HyperStudio CD supports Pioneer models only.

- Your laserdisc player must be connected to the computer with a CC04 cable. This cable connects the laserdisc player to the modem or printer port of your computer. Remember that electrical connections can be loose. Sometimes the solution can be as simple as jiggling the cord! If you are using a Quadra 660AV, check the Express Modem control panel. The correct settings are "External modem" and "Express Modem Off".

- You are connected to the printer port. Although you can control a laserdisc player which is connected to the printer port, HyperStudio must be told that you are connected to it. From the Extras menu, choose the Laserdisc Port Chooser to tell HyperStudio that you are using the Printer port.

- The small configuration switches of the laserdisc player need to be set correctly. On Pioneer models 2200, 2400 and 2600, all switches should be set to off. On the 4400 model switch 1 must be off, and switch 2 must be on.

If you can see HyperStudio's laserdisc control panel, but no video window you should check the following:

- If you are using a TV-style monitor to display the laserdisc image, a standard video ("RCA") cable must connect the "video out" of the laserdisc player to the "video in" of the TV monitor. Alternatively, you can also use an antenna-style wire ("coax cable"). In either case, make sure that your TV is set to channel 3 or 4 as corresponds to the switch on the laserdisc player, or that the TV is set to "video" if you're using the direct video connection.

- If the connections look correct, the cable itself might be defective, so changing the cable could solve the problem.

- If you are using HyperStudio on an "AV" Mac or using a video digitizing device such as "Movie-Movie", you can actually display the laserdisc image right on your computer screen! If you have such a setup, and can't see the video image on your screen when you use the "Viewer" checkbox, make sure that the video cable goes from the "video out" of the laserdisc player to the "video in" of the computer digitizer. PowerMacs may require a small adapter cable to match the small RCA-style connector to the 4-pin S-Video input of the PowerMac AV cards.

"I thought HyperStudio could capture images directly from a video camera. How do I do that?"

The first requirement is that you have a video digitizer in your computer. This is built-in on "AV" Macs, and HyperStudio supports this feature directly through Add Clip-Art and other image-loading functions. If you have an add-on digitizer, such as the Movie-

Movie card, ComputerEyes/RT, or the Connectix QuickCam, and have installed the driver software, then HyperStudio will automatically recognize these as well. Some digitizers, such as the Video Spigot, do not have the proper driver files ("VDIG files") to be used within HyperStudio. In those cases, you'll have to use the software that comes with the device, capture the image or movies, and then save them to a disk. The image can then be brought into HyperStudio with Add Clip-Art, etc. from disk.

> **NOTE:** If you have the QuickTake camera, no video digitizer is required. Just install the software, and HyperStudio's "Add Clip-Art" will do the rest!

"The stack I have opened has a shortened menu bar. How can I get all the menus back?"

If you have not specifically locked the stack you are looking at, what has probably happened is that you have used the HyperStudio Player to open your stack, rather than the full version. The Player version of HyperStudio is the version you can put on a disk with your stacks when sharing projects with others who don't own a copy of the program. This player allows viewing of projects, but does not have any authoring capabilities.

When you double-click on a stack to open it from the Finder, the full version of HyperStudio should be launched. However, if for some reason the HyperStudio Player was launched, you can do either of the following:

Rebuild your Desktop by pressing the option and command keys while you restart your computer. This may return your system to running HyperStudio when you double-click on a stack. If not...

Drag the Player from the My Stacks folder onto a floppy disk as a "parking place" for future use, and then go back and drag Player into the Trash.

"When I run HyperStudio on some Macs, some stacks display the message 'Converting'. Why is this?"

If the computer you are using only supports 256 colors (or only black and white), and you are trying to view a 16-color stack, HyperStudio will attempt to convert the color level of the stack. If the situation is temporary, then just let it convert the stack, and view it in that environment. However, if you would like to avoid this conversion in the future, then use Save As to save the converted stack back over the original, using the same name as the original, and replace the 16-color version of the stack with the 256-color (or black & white) version.

"When I move my stacks from the computer on which they were made to another computer, messages appear unexpectedly that tell me to insert a disk with the name of my original hard disk. Why is this?"

Generally speaking, all text, sounds and graphics are moved right into your stack as you create your project. This way, there is just one file to deal with when you move from one disk to another. However, there is an exception to this: QuickTime movies.

QuickTime movies are so frequently of a large size, that HyperStudio sets up just a pointer to the movie when you make a button that plays a movie. It would be impractical to store, for example, a 4 Mb movie within a 500k stack. However, this means that if your stack accesses a QuickTime movie file, you'll have to remember to move the movie file as well as your stack to the new location. When doing this, the easiest approach is to just put any QuickTime movies that your stack needs in the same folder as your stack on the destination computer

Advanced Technique: Disk-based Sounds, Graphics and Text

If you have marked the HyperStudio Preferences as an "I'm an experienced HyperStudio user", then you have the option of marking sounds, graphics and text items as "disk-based". What this means is that this data will now be treated like QuickTime movies. That is, HyperStudio will just remember where the original file is with a "pointer", rather than store the data within the stack. This has the advantage of keeping your stack small, and lets others change the data from outside the stack. However, it is now up to you to remember to move those sound, text, or graphics files with your stack when you move your project to another computer.

Remember that in all cases where HyperStudio can't find a file, and prompts you to insert the original disk on which the data was located, it will also let you know that it is looking, for example, for a "sound file named Drama1". This information can be very useful in figuring out which file was left behind when a stack was moved.

Index

Index

Index

HyperStudio®
Software for a Mediacentric World!

Contents

HyperStudio®
Software for a Mediacentric World!

Getting Started

In this chapter:

HyperStudio gives you control over the computer screen, rather than the computer screen having control over you. That's what makes HyperStudio so much fun! This chapter will introduce you to HyperStudio's guide dog, Addy, and will explain some of the conventions used throughout the tutorial.

Imagine...

Making a game with questions, answers, sound effects and scoring!

Making presentations on anything from archeology to zoology!

Teaching anything from colors to calculus!

Making a journal of your travels filled with maps, photos and comments!

Creating characters and caricatures in the paint program!

Writing animated fictional stories or documenting historical events with video from laserdisc and QuickTime Movies!

Creating your résumé complete with your voice, pictures of how you improved your work place and of books you've written!

Having so much fun with your computer!

HyperStudio!

The idea behind HyperStudio

Home Stack

With HyperStudio you'll create **cards**. A series of cards is called a **stack**. Your project can be a single stack, or many stacks which have been linked together.

You can use the **paint tools** and draw on the background of the card.
You can also add pre-drawn art or **clip-art** and **graphics** from the HyperStudio Art folder, other CD-ROMs or even the Internet!

You can add **text objects** (write on the card)
You can get text files from other sources as well.

You can add **sound** to the card. You can record your own voice, use the prerecorded sounds which come with HyperStudio, and access audio CDs.

Buttons are hot spots on the screen where you click the mouse to make things happen.

You can play **laserdiscs and CDs.**

You can record, edit and show **QuickTime** movies.

Meet Addy!

HyperStudio is a very "conversational" program. It talks to you while you're using it. When you begin a new project, other programs would leave you staring at a blank screen. If you've ever watched a new user with a computer it is not until they see "Untitled 17" that they realize what's been happening. In HyperStudio, the first time that you start a new stack, you'll meet our helpful guide, Addy. Throughout the program, Addy will appear in dialog boxes to help you out and guide you along your way as you use the software. However, Addy is also a polite guide, and so you'll notice that the second time you start a project in a given session with HyperStudio, you'll be delivered right to the first card without seeing the explanatory note.

Addy is more than just a regular dog. She knows that people, just like dogs, have different personalities. She wants to be sure that you'll get everything that you want out of this manual and the program. If you are the orderly-sequential type, you'll like the step-by-step instructions for creating a project about France in Chapter 3. If you're the exploratory type, then HyperStudio as an environment is very friendly to experimentation and discovery. You will probably enjoy browsing the reference manual to get a general idea of what's available, then returning to it as needed, when your adventures require a little extra assistance.

With either approach, once you have become comfortable with the basics of HyperStudio, the Tips and Techniques in chapter 3, the advanced techniques in chapter 4 and the Ask Addy chapter will show you things that will make you an even better HyperStudio user.

Important Stuff!

❖ These are the Menu titles in ——— HyperStudio:

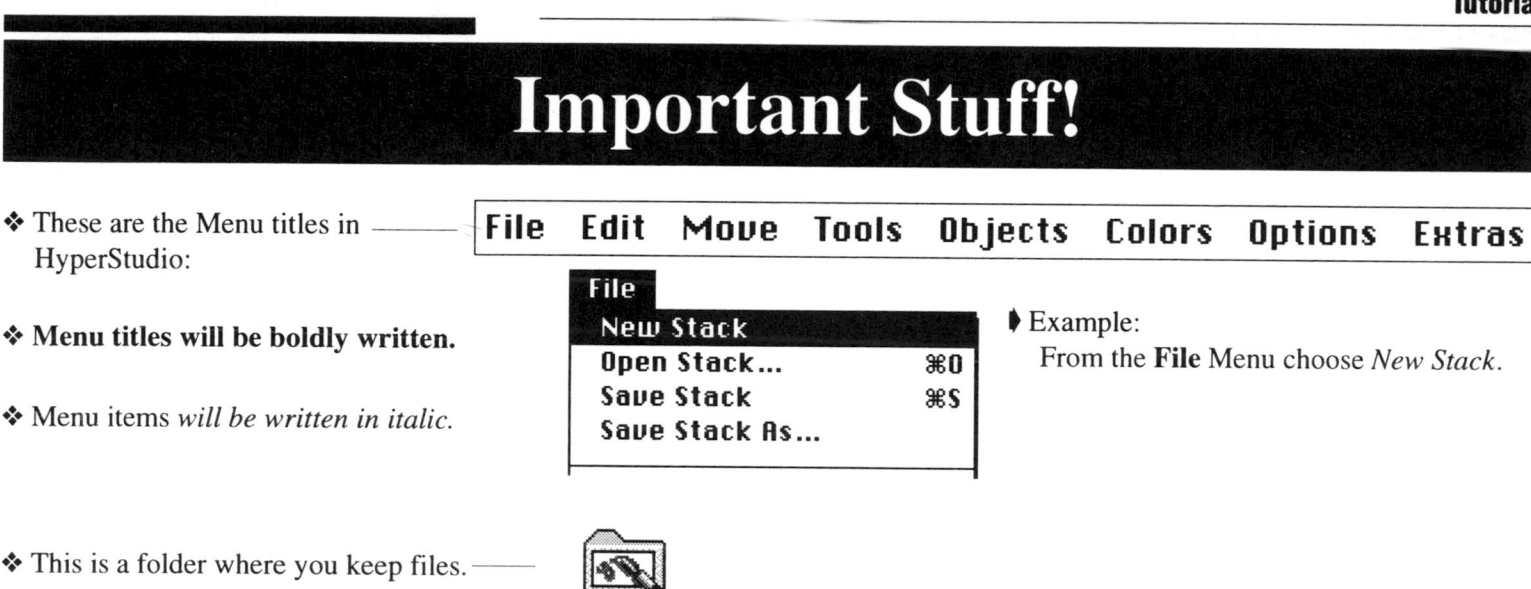

| File Edit Move Tools Objects Colors Options Extras |

❖ **Menu titles will be boldly written.**

❖ Menu items *will be written in italic.*

File
New Stack
Open Stack...   ⌘O
Save Stack   ⌘S
Save Stack As...

▶ Example:
  From the **File** Menu choose *New Stack.*

❖ This is a folder where you keep files. ———

HS Art

❖ These are files kept inside a folder. ———

Animals   Home Stack

❖ File names will be
  written like this.

⬚ **HyperStudio** ▼
⬚ Demo
⬚ Adventure stack
⬚ Animal Book
☐ **Animation Stuff**
⬚ Bobcats
⬚ Brown Is Brown

⬚Macint...
[Eject]
[Desktop]

Please name this STACK:
France

[Save]
[Cancel]

▶ Example: When you save your stack, give
  it the name: France.

The Paint Tools

In this chapter:

This chapter will help you become familiar with the paint tools in HyperStudio. The step-by-step tutorial in Chapter 3 for creating a project on France assumes that you are comfortable with the mouse, the eraser and the selector tool. If you haven't used a paint program before, you should spend some time experimenting with the different tools.

Tearing Away the Tools Menu

▶ A neat feature of HyperStudio is being able to "tear off" the **Tools** and **Colors** menus. This lets you place the menu on the card so that you may choose a tool without pulling down the **Tools** menu each time, and choose a color without pulling down the **Colors** menu.

▶ To tear away the Tools menu drag the mouse down and past the tools, without releasing the mouse button, until you can see that the tool palette has been torn away.

▶ The Tools menu can be repositioned on the screen by dragging the grey bar across the top.

▶ To put the tools menu away click in the small square window at the top left corner of the palette.

▶ You can tear away the **Colors** menu, and then put it away later in the same manner.

Tips about the Shift Key

▶ Pressing *shift* while you draw with the Pencil tool   or the Paint Brush   is a little trick for drawing straight lines!

▶ If you press the *shift* key while you use the Spray Can   , you can spray paint in a straight line!

▶ If you press the *shift* key while you use the eraser, you can erase in a straight line!

▶ Pressing the *shift* key while you use the ◯ will draw circles.

▶ Pressing the *shift* key while you use the ☐ will draw squares.

Tips about the Selector Tool

▶ To use the ⸢⸤ , position the mouse at the upper left-hand corner of the image you want to

select and drag the mouse diagonally down to just past the lower right-hand corner of the image. When selecting something, you'll notice flashing dots outlining the area selected. If you didn't select the area properly, you can click outside the flashing dots to turn them off and try again!

Different Lines, Colors, and Paint Brushes

▶ You can choose different line thicknesses for your lines, rectangles and ovals by choosing *Line Size* from the **Options** menu.

▶ You can choose different colors from the **Colors** menu.

▶ You can choose different brush shapes from the **Options** menu.

The Paint Tools Illustrated

● Circular Selector
This tool lets you capture an oval area. Circular or oval pictures can be used as buttons or cameo-style photos.

● Lasso
Outline a shape with this tool and it will hug the shape so you can copy it, cut it, delete it, move it, or resize it.

● Square Selector
This tool lets you capture a rectangular area. Now you can copy it, cut it, delete it, move it, flip it, rotate it or resize it.

● Paint can
Use this fill tool to color a closed shape.

● Paintbrush
Draw freehand using one of many different brush shapes.

● Spraypaint
Scatter lots of tiny dots with this tool.

● Eraser
Set the eraser color and erase!

● Pencil
Draw freehand.

● Line Tool
Draws straight lines.

● Rectangle
Use this tool to draw rectangles and squares.

● Rounded Rectangle
Use this tool to draw rounded rectangles and squares.

● Oval
Use this tool to draw ovals and circles.

● Eye Dropper
Use this tool when you want to know what a particular color is, so you can paint with it somewhere else

● Paint Text
Paint text on a card with this tool.

● Magnifying Glass
Zooms you in closer.
All the paint tools work there, too.

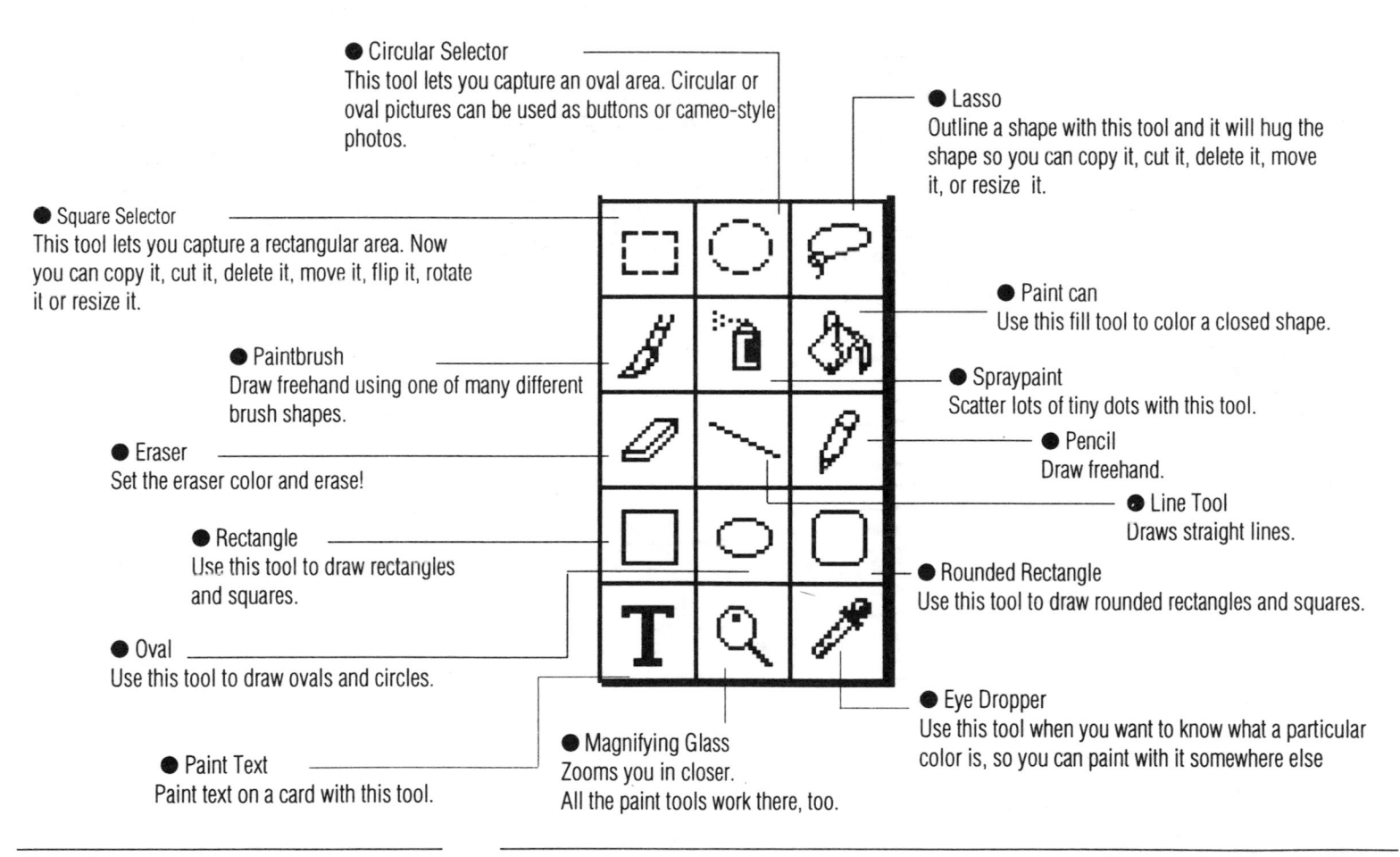

Tips on How to Erase

To erase painted images or text, you have several options:

❶ Use the eraser tool.

❷ Use the ⌐¬ . Select the part you'd like to erase and once you see the flashing dots, press the *delete* key.

❸ Immediately after you draw something, you can choose *Undo painting* (from the **Edit** menu), or use the keyboard shortcut, pressing ⌘-Z. (While you hold down the ⌘ key, press the Z once.) Try drawing a line and right after that pressing ⌘-Z. If you happen to click on the 🖱 before you press ⌘-Z, it will be too late to *Undo* it.

❹ From the **Edit** menu, choose *Erase Background*. This will erase your whole background and make your card the color you select.

Tip on Painting Text

▶ You can edit the text, use the delete key, choose a different color, size and font before you click away from the painted text typed with the T tool. Once you click the mouse away from the text you have just painted with the T tool, you will have lost the ability to make changes to that text so easily. It's a good idea to check your text carefully before clicking the mouse. You will be learning about Text Objects (in the step-by-step project), for text that can be easily edited.

This activity can be done using the paint tools: (See the illustration on the opposite page.)

To Begin:

❏ Choose New Stack from the **File** menu. This will give you a blank card on which you can create this project.

To Change the Color of the Card:

❏ Choose Erase Background... from the **Edit** menu. Choose yellow.
❏ Click on OK.

To Draw a Border:

❏ From the **Options** menu choose Line Size.
❏ Choose the third line thickness then click on OK.
❏ From the Colors menu, choose bright blue.
❏ Using the Rectangle tool (□) begin at the top left-hand corner and drag diagonally down and to the right, until the rectangle creates a border. Release the mouse.

To Paint Text:

❏ From the **Options** menu, choose Text Style. Choose Chicago 24, bright blue. Click on OK.
❏ Choose the T tool. The cursor will change to a text cursor.
❏ Set the cursor down where you want to begin writing the text. Be sure to leave enough room for the cursor to clear the border you have drawn. Set the cursor down one half inch to the right of the border and an inch below it.
❏ Type "If you are a police dog, (Press return to get to a new line.) where's your badge?"

❏ Check your spelling before you click away from the text as you cannot use the delete key to delete letters once you click away from this text.

To Move the Painted Text:

❏ Use the Selector tool to reposition the text. To do this select a rectangular area around the quote. When you see the flashing dots, drag the selected area to the new position. When positioned over the selected area the cursor becomes a 4-way directional arrow to let you know that you can drag the area. Click away from the flashing dots to place the selected area.

❏ Using the T tool type "James Thurber".

❏ Position his name in the lower right-hand area of the card.

That's it! You are ready to start a HyperStudio project.
We will not save this card.

Untitled - Card 1

"If you are a police dog, where's your badge?"

James Thurber

Use: To :

☝ Remember:

✓ You can begin your selection by clicking somewhere else on the card to turn off the flashing dots, and then try again.

✓ Move the mouse carefully across the flashing dots, to wait for the 4-way directional arrow, **before** you drag the mouse to move or copy the image.

✓ Which ever color is on the outside while you lasso something, will be transparent on the inside when you move it. Example: Yellow school bus, on white background with white windows - the windows will be transparent. (In the picture to the left, the inside of the hoop will be transparent.)

✓ The circular selector is a great tool for creating cameo-style pictures.

✓ Pressing *shift* will select circles.

Use: To :

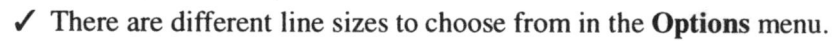

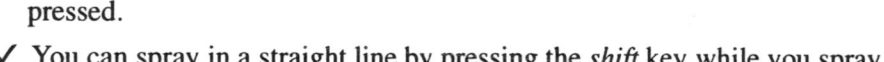

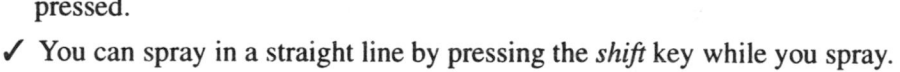

☝ Remember:

✓ There are lots of brush shapes to choose from in the **Options** menu.

✓ You can erase against a straight edge by pressing *shift* while you erase.

✓ There are different line sizes to choose from in the **Options** menu.

✓ You can spray a heavier concentration of dots, by keeping the mouse button pressed.

✓ You can spray in a straight line by pressing the *shift* key while you spray.

Use: To :    Remember:

    ☐   ✓ Pressing *shift* will draw squares.

☐   ☐   ✓ Pressing *shift* will draw squares with rounded corners.

    🍎   ✓ Aim the "hot spot" of the paint can in an enclosed area.

     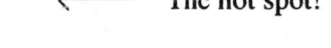 The hot spot!

☐   👀   ✓ Pressing *shift* will draw circles.

Use: To :

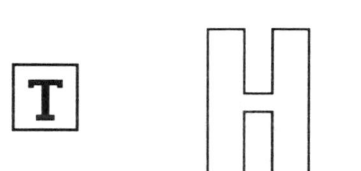

👆 Remember:

✓ This text can be edited and changed easily **before** the mouse is clicked.

✓ Press *return* to begin a new line.

✓ This is for painted text!

✓ HyperStudio can zoom in at 100%, 200%, 400% and 800%.

✓ All the paint tools work in the Magnify mode.

✓ Press the *esc* key to return to normal magnification.

✓ Use the eye dropper to pick up a color which you may want to use somewhere else.

✓ ⌘ - click with the pencil will pick a color right off the screen, without pulling down the **Colors** menu. This is like using the eye dropper to pick up a color.

Creating a Project

In this chapter:

Follow the step-by-step instructions to create your first HyperStudio project.

You might want to refer to the tips and techniques on the left-hand pages even after you have become an experienced HyperStudio user!

Points to Ponder

It is impossible to overstate the enormity of changes in literacy and literacy practices wrought by developments in electronic technologies. Because we can't comprehend what is happening, we search for apt metaphors, or for historical examples which might serve to explain what is happening. So let me ask: "Are we in the middle of a second Gutenberg revolution?" The answer is: "No, we're not"; what is taking place in the field of literacy is more far-reaching, and more fundamental.

- Gunther Kress

Preface A-Z 21st Century Literacy Handbook

As the publishing and entertainment industries are rushing to deliver information in a multimedia, CD-ROM form, now is the time to prepare to become effective communicators in this new style of expression and information. HyperStudio is a creative environment where users can bring graphics, sound, and text together in a simple, intuitive and exciting way. The goal of this tutorial is to learn the basic skills needed to use HyperStudio. By creating this project we hope you'll see how creative multimedia gives you some very important and powerful tools with which to express yourself.

The Way to Use this Tutorial

The **right-hand pages are the action pages**. Follow these directions carefully. Use the little checkboxes (❑) to keep track of what you have completed. The **left-hand pages are filled with "Tips and Techniques"**. These will be referenced on the action pages. Refer to the tips as your interest dictates, and then return to the action page.

About this Project

We will be creating a four-card stack. We have chosen a project on France, as this touches on many possible themes: travel, business, family history and school projects. On the title card you will learn how to get a **border** from the HyperStudio clip art folder. You will be adding a **digitized picture**. This will be one provided in HyperStudio, or can be your own if you are working on an AV Mac, have a digitizer such as ComputerEyes/RT, or have a QuickTake camera. This digitized picture could in fact be one of salespeople, a corporate office, a student, or a company or school logo. A **button** which includes the **sound** of your voice will take you to card two. On the second card, you will add a map of Europe and an invisible button to take you to card three. We will go back and add enhancements to card two as your skills improve. On Card three you will add a **text object** with some **text**, and a **graphic object** of a street artist which will appear at the click of the phrase in the text object, a **hypertext link**. Finally we will add a ready-made card of a bibliography template. Once we are done, we will return to card three to play a **QuickTime movie** and then to card two to create an **animation**. The Going Further section will teach you how to play QuickTime movies in irregular shapes and use gradients for the title on Card 1.

A Word about Stack Design

This book suggests only one method of creating a four-card stack. There isn't really an incorrect way to do this. As you use HyperStudio, you will develop your own style. Whether you create several cards and then make the buttons to connect them, or create the buttons along the way, will eventually be up to you.

Stacks can be **linear**, such as in a book where the cards are connected sequentially. Other projects can use the **branching** method, where one card (like a Table of Contents) connects to cards throughout the stack. A **circular** style stack might be used for projects which demonstrate cycles.

A Look at the Project...

Card 1

- The Circular Selector Tool was used to create this cameo-style photograph.
- The Let's Go! button will take you to card 2, the map of Europe.

Card 2

- Click on the word "France" to see it move across the map and finally stop over the country, France.
- Click on France, the country, (an invisible button) to take you to card 3.

If you would like to see a completed example of this project, open the stack called "Tutorial Project" located on the HyperStudio CD (look in the "Sample Projects" folder for this stack).

Card 3

- This portion of the map has been copied from card 2 and pasted here.

- Click on the film strip to see the QuickTime movie. The Going Further section explains how to play the movie in the shape of France!

- This text object contains the phrase "street artist". Clicking on that phrase will display the graphic of the street artist!

- Click on the icon of the mouse to get to the Bibliography card.

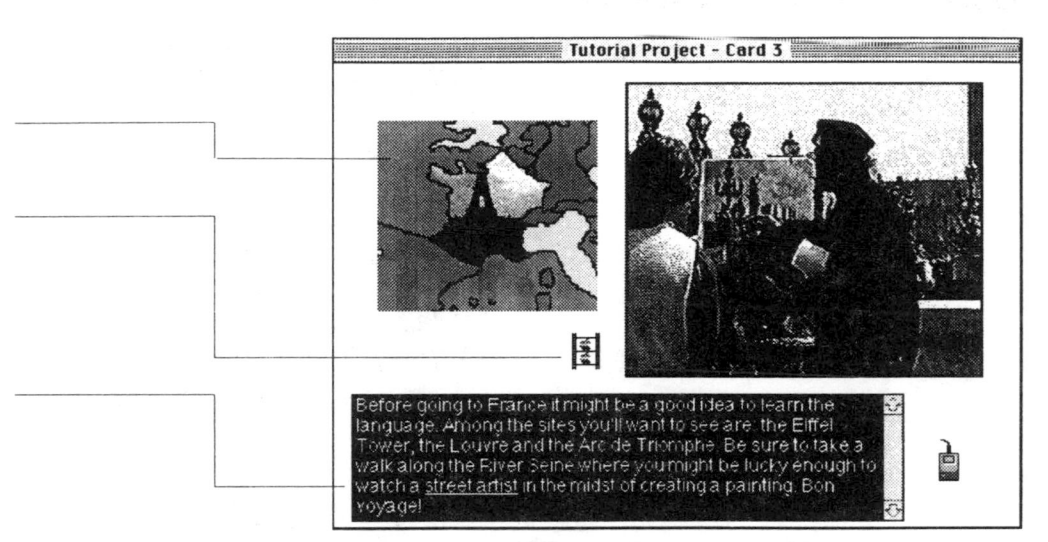

Card 4

- This Bibliography is a Ready-Made Card Template which is part of the HyperStudio package. It is a good idea to end all projects with this card, and fill in the appropriate information!

Tip #1:

Changing to a 16-Color Stack

When you are not playing QuickTime movies or adding digitized pictures to a stack, and memory is a concern, it is a good idea to work in the 16-color mode. To convert a stack to 16 colors, you would follow these four steps. (This is for your information only. There is no need to convert the stack now.)

▶ From the **Objects** menu choose *About this Stack*. (Fig. 1)

▶ Click on Change # of colors or size... (Fig.2)

▶ Choose 16 colors and then click on OK. (Fig. 3)

▶ Click on OK at the About stack screen (Fig. 2)

Tip #2:

When an Area is Selected

with the Selector Tool

▶ You can **move** the selected area by placing the mouse within the selected area and dragging the mouse to a new position.

▶ You can **erase** the selected area by pressing the delete key.

▶ You can **make a copy** of the selected area by pressing the option key as you drag the mouse.

▶ You can **resize** the image by grabbing the lower-right-hand corner of the selected area and dragging the mouse. (The cursor will switch to a two-headed diagonal arrow.)

▶ You can **place or drop** the selected area on the card by clicking outside of the selected area. Clicking outside an area without moving it just de-selects the area.

Tip #3:

Make a Mistake?

▶ Choose *Undo* from the **Edit** menu, or press the Command key ⌘ and the letter Z.

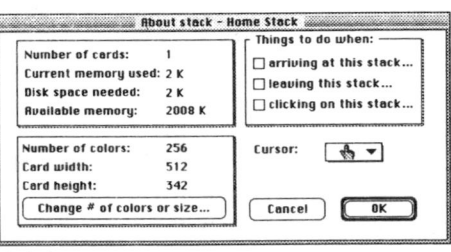

Objects

Add a Button...	⌘B
Add a Graphic Object...	⌘G
Add a Text Object...	⌘T
Hypertext Links...	⌘L
Bring Closer	⌘+
Send Farther	⌘−
About this Card...	
About this Stack...	

▲▲▲

Figure 1: Objects menu

About stack - Home Stack

Number of cards:	1
Current memory used:	2 K
Disk space needed:	2 K
Available memory:	2008 K

Things to do when:
☐ arriving at this stack...
☐ leaving this stack...
☐ clicking on this stack...

Number of colors:	256
Card width:	512
Card height:	342

Cursor: [☞ ▼]

[Change # of colors or size...]   [Cancel]   [OK]

▲▲▲

Figure 2: About This Stack... dialog

Figure 3: Number of colors & card size

▼▼▼

Pick how many colors you want and how big
you want your cards to be (or just click OK).

Pick how many colors:
○ Black and white
○ 16 colors
◉ 256 colors

Pick a card size:
[Standard HyperStudio Card ▼]

Width 512   Height 342

[Cancel]   [OK]

Beginning Your Project

☐ From the **File** menu (Fig. 4) choose *New Stack*. This will give you the first card on which you can start building your project.
☐ There are times that you might want to work in a 16-color stack. (See Tip #1, page 24)

Adding a Border

We will be importing a background, and then deleting its center.

☐ From the **File** menu (Fig. 4) choose *Import Background*.
☐ Choose Disk File when you see the message (Fig. 5) and click on OK. If you do not have a QuickTake camera installed or a video digitizer, you will not see this message.
☐ From the HS Art folder, choose `Dingbats 2`.
☐ Click on Open.
☐ Dingbats 2 should be covering Card 1.
☐ From the **Tools** menu (Fig. 6) choose the *Selector tool*.
☐ Practice using it to select an area. To do this begin above and to the left of the area you want to capture, and drag the mouse diagonally down and to the right, past the area you want to select. While you see the flashing dots, the area is selected. (See Tip #2, page 24)
☐ Press the delete key to erase the selected area. (See Tip #3, page 24)
☐ Using the selector tool delete the center section of the card, leaving the border only.

Adding a Digitized Picture

Tip #4:

Adding a Picture to a Stack

HyperStudio gives you three options when you Add Clip Art, Load a Background, or Add a Graphic Object to a card. You can either:

✓ get the already digitized image from Disk file, which means that the file is on the hard drive, a floppy disk or a CD.

✓ let HyperStudio instantly digitize an image from a camcorder, VCR, or laserdisc player by choosing the "Video" option. In this case your camcorder must be connected to the "Video In" of your computer. (You must be working on either a Mac AV or be using a digitizer such as ComputerEyes/RT, or the Connectix QuickCam.)

✓ attach your QuickTake camera and let HyperStudio go directly to the camera to show you thumbnails of the pictures you have taken. You can choose the picture you want without having to use any of the QuickTake software or Desk Accessories.

Tip #5:

When you are Adding Clip Art

◗ If you are selecting something which is taller than the clip art window (such as one of the columns in Dingbats 2), here is some advice. Start at the upper left of the column and drag down as you select. When you reach the edge of the window, keep dragging. It will automatically scroll to allow you to select more of the screen.

Tip # 6:

The Circular Selector Tool

and Perfect Circles

◗ The circular selector tool will give you an oval. Holding down the shift key will give you a circle.

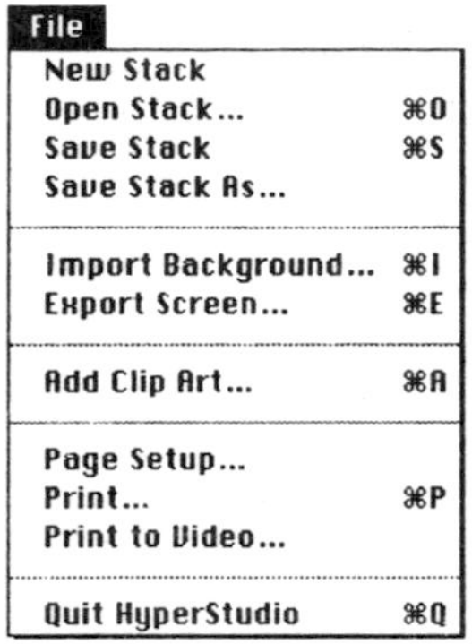

File

New Stack	
Open Stack...	⌘O
Save Stack	⌘S
Save Stack As...	
Import Background...	⌘I
Export Screen...	⌘E
Add Clip Art...	⌘A
Page Setup...	
Print...	⌘P
Print to Video...	
Quit HyperStudio	⌘Q

▲▲▲
Figure 4: File Menu

Figure 5: Picture source dialog
▼▼▼

Where do you want to get your picture from?
- ● Disk file
- ○ Video
- ○ QuickTake camera

[Cancel] [OK]

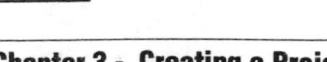
◀◀◀ *Figure 6: The Tools Menu*

We will be adding a picture from the Photos folder, but you can make your own now if you have a QuickTake camera or Mac AV. (See Tip # 4, page 26)

❏ From the **File** menu (Fig. 4), choose Add Clip Art.

❏ If you have a video digitizer or QuickTake installed, but aren't using it now, then choose Disk file and then click on OK. (See Fig. 5)

❏ From the HS Art folder, choose the Photos folder, and within that, the "Boy with Boats" picture, a digitized photograph.

❏ Using the selector tool, select about a two or three inch square of the picture. Start a little to the left and top of the tallest tree (on the left of the picture) and drag diagonally down and to the right until you have selected the image of the boy and the boats. (See Tip #5, page 26)

❏ Click on OK.

❏ Drag the picture toward the bottom right-hand area of the card. Click away from the flashing dots to place the picture. Do not cover the border.

Creating a Cameo

❏ To cut a cameo from the photograph, choose the Circlular Selector tool from the Tools menu.

❏ Begin above and to the left of the area you want to select, and drag diagonally down and to the right, until you have a pleasing oval. Click away from the flashing dots to turn them off if you need to try again. (See Tip #6, page 26)

❏ Once you have a nice area selected, do not click away from the flashing dots.

❏ As you move the cursor across the oval, it will become a 4-way directional arrow. It is with this arrow that you can drag the selected image. Drag it

Tip #7:

Using the T Tool

▶ You can edit the text, use the delete key, change the color, size and font **before** you click away from painted text typed with the T tool. Please check your title and spelling before you click away from the last character you typed.

▶ You can move the painted text by selecting it with the selector tool and then dragging the selected image to a new position on the card.

Tip #8:

Saving

▶ Use Save Stack As...the first time you save a project or when you want to make a backup under another name.

▶ Once you save, the stack name will appear at the top of your card.

▶ Once it has been saved, you can choose Save Stack from the File menu, or the keyboard shortcut ⌘-S.

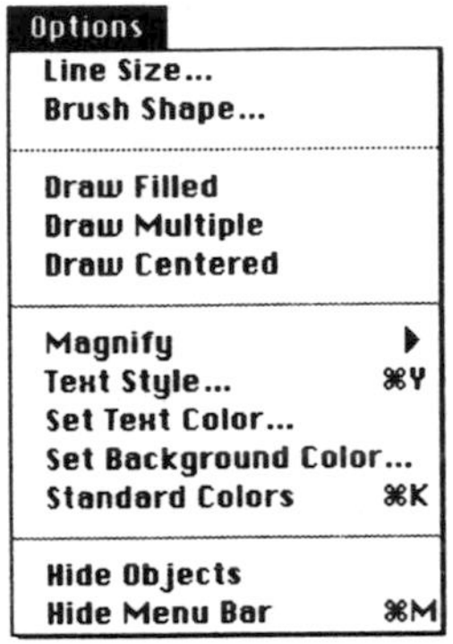

Options

Line Size...
Brush Shape...

Draw Filled
Draw Multiple
Draw Centered

Magnify   ▶
Text Style...   ⌘Y
Set Text Color...
Set Background Color...
Standard Colors   ⌘K

Hide Objects
Hide Menu Bar   ⌘M

▲▲▲

Figure 7: Options Menu

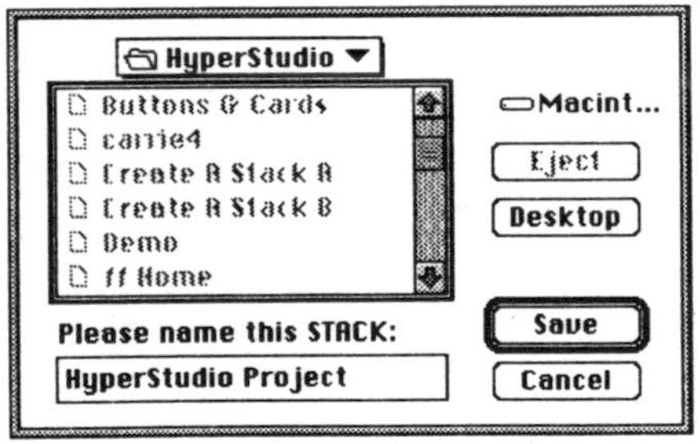

Figure 8: The "Save As..." dialog.

away from the original photograph and move it to the lower-left side of the card. Click away from the flashing dots to place the image.

❑ Using the square selector tool, select the remainder of the picture, and then press the delete key to remove it from the card.

Adding a Title to the Card

We will be painting a title on the background of this card.

❑ From the **Options** menu (Fig. 7) choose *Text Style*.

❑ Choose Times, Bold, Size 72, medium blue. Click on OK.

❑ Choose the *T (Text tool)* from the **Tools** menu. (Fig. 6)

❑ The cursor will change to a text cursor. Set the cursor down on the card by clicking the mouse where you want the first character. Allow enough space for the total height of the character you will be typing. Begin one inch below the border and two inches to the right of it.

❑ Type the title, France. (See Tip #7, page 28)

Saving Your Stack

We'll be saving the project on the Desktop.

❑ From the **File** menu, choose *Save Stack As...* (Fig. 4)

❑ Save your stack on the Desktop, by clicking the Desktop button. (You can drag the stack onto a data disk later on.)

❑ Name the stack HyperStudio Project. (Fig. 8)

❑ Click on Save. (See Tip #8, page 28)

Adding a Second Card to Your Stack

Tip # 9:

Adding New Cards

to a Stack

▶ Don't worry when adding a new card to your stack and the one you were looking at seems to disappear; your other card(s) will still be there.

▶ When you add a new card, it is added right after the card you are *currently* looking at.

▶ Your stack can contain an unlimited number of cards, but it is a better idea to keep the number of cards within a stack manageable. Five to ten cards per stack is a good number. You can button these smaller stacks together, like chapters in a book. Use "connect to another stack" in the Actions dialog box.

Tip #10:

Moving Manually

Through a Stack

▶ Before you create buttons, there are menu items and keyboard shortcuts which will allow you to move around in your stack. From the Move menu, you could have chosen; Move Back (⌘ -~), Move First Card (⌘ -1), Move Next Card, (⌘ ->), or Move Back (⌘ -<), to get back to Card 1 from Card 2 . The good news here is it's pretty difficult to get lost in a two-card stack!

Edit

Undo	⌘Z
Cut	⌘H
Copy	⌘C
Paste text	⌘U
Clear	
New Card	⌘N
Ready Made Cards	▶
Delete Card	
Cut Card	
Copy Card	
Edit this Object...	
Effects	▶
Erase Background...	
Preferences	⌘;

▲▲▲

Figure 9: Edit Menu

Figure 10: Selecting "HS Art" folder
▼▼▼

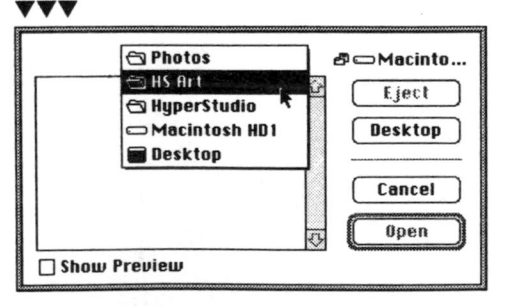

❑ From the **Edit** menu (Fig. 9) choose *New Card*. (See Tip #9, page 30)

Importing a Background for the Entire Card

❑ Choose *Import Background* from the **File** menu. (Fig. 4)

❑ You'll get the message asking where you want to get the picture from if you have a video digitizer or the QuickTake software installed. Click on Disk file and OK. (Fig. 5)

❑ You'll be in the Photos folder. To get back to the HS Art folder use the directories list at the top of the dialog box. Choose HS Art. (Fig. 10)

❑ From the HS Art folder choose Europe.

❑ Click on Open.

❑ The map of Europe should be on card 2.

Moving Back to Card 1

❑ To move back to the first card in the stack, choose *Previous Card* from the **Move** menu. You can use the keyboard shortcut ⌘-<. (See Tip #10, Page 30)

Tip #11:

Button Stuff

▶ Buttons are places on the screen where you click to make things happen. When you create a button, HyperStudio wants to know 3 things:

❶ What the button should look like.

❷ Where you want it.

❸ What it will do.

▶ Do not use the double-ringed visible button on a card where there is a text item, because this type of button is activated by pressing the return key.

Tip # 12:

Help Messages

When you Make a Button

▶ When you make a button for the first time, HyperStudio will put up a help screen reminding you of the procedure for making a button, if you do not have "I'm an experienced HyperStudio user" checked in the Preferences.

Tip #13:

Transitions

▶ You can create some really neat effects by using certain transitions for a button. You can have new text revealed if you use a "Left to Right" transition. Things can seem to appear magically when you use the transition titled *Dissolve*.

Figure 11: Button Appearance dialog
▼▼▼

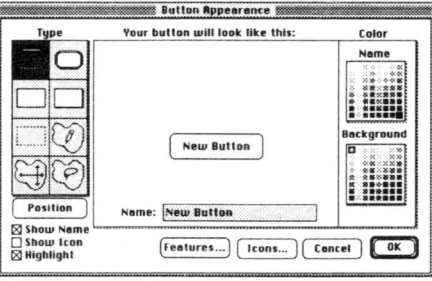

Figure 12: Selecting an icon for the button
▼▼▼

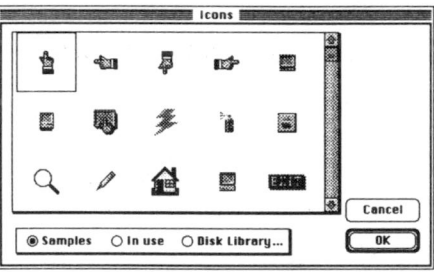

Figure 13: The Actions dialog
▼▼▼

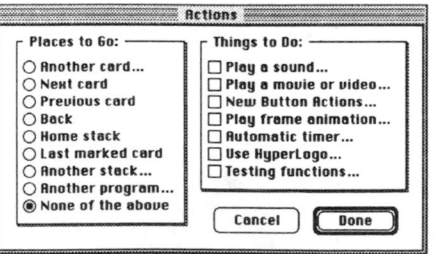

Making a Visible Button to Connect Two Cards

We'll be creating a button with an icon to link the two cards. We'll then edit the button (a useful skill) to add some sound.

❑ To make a button choose *Add a Button* from the **Objects** menu. (Fig.1) (See Tip #11, Page 32)

❑ At the Button Appearance screen (Fig. 11) choose the rectangular button with the shadow. Write the name "Let's Go!" Click on medium blue for the name of the button, and click on yellow for the background color of the button.

❑ Click on Icons to select an icon for the button. (Fig. 12)

❑ Select the icon of the hand pointing toward the right.

❑ Click on OK.

❑ Click on OK at the Button Appearance menu.

❑ An instruction screen will appear. Click on OK. (see Tip# 12, page 32)

❑ You'll see the button floating over the card and waiting to be placed.

❑ Drag the button to the bottom-right-hand corner of the card, just next to the border.

❑ Click outside the flashing dots to place the button there.

❑ As soon as you click away from the button, you will see the Actions screen. (Fig. 13)

❑ On the Places To Go side click on Next Card. This will automatically take you to the Transitions screen (Fig.14) where you can choose the visual effect you want to use to take you to Card 2. (See Tip #13, page 32.)

❑ Choose Barn Open (you'll have to scroll down a bit to see it). Clicking on Try It will allow you to see what the sequence will look like. Then Click on OK.

❑ This will bring you back to the Actions screen. (Fig. 13)

❑ Click on Done. (Your button is now complete.)

Tip #14:

Editing Buttons

- If you create a button and then want to move it, delete it, or change what it does, you can use the Arrow tool.

- Use the Arrow tool to edit a button and use the Browse tool to navigate your way through a stack.

- Be sure to switch back to the Browse tool after you have edited a button.

- Pressing shift - tab will toggle back and forth between the Browse and Editing (arrow) tools.

Tip #15:

Recording Sounds

- While you are recording, the "gas gauge" will move showing the memory you are using up while recording. It's a good idea to be prepared with what you want to say before you click on the Record button.

- If sound quality is important, you can hold down the Command ( ) key when you first click the Record button on the screen. This will give clearer recordings, but does use twice as much memory. In a noisy classroom the added quality is probably not needed. However, for an auditorium presentation, you may find the Command key variation useful!

Tip #16:

Sample Sounds

- Sounds that show up in the Samples list are stored in the stack HS Samples Library. If you move the HyperStudio application and you don't take that stack (HS Samples Library) with you, you will get an error message. If you want to change the sample sounds, you can open the HS Samples Library stack and add or delete any sounds you wish.

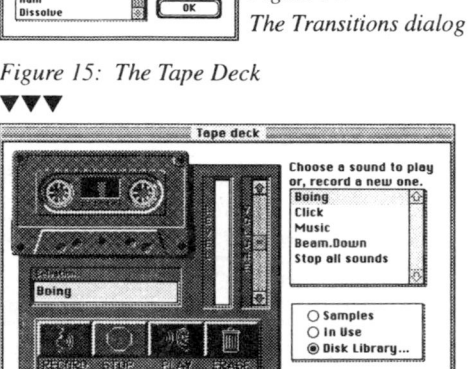

Figure 14:
The Transitions dialog

Figure 15: The Tape Deck

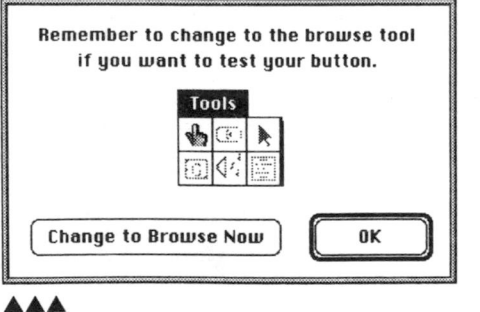
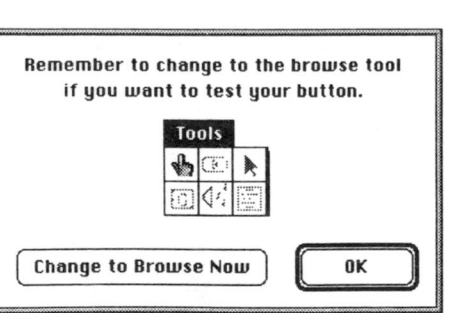

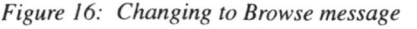

Figure 16: Changing to Browse message

❏ Click on your button to try it out.
❏ Once you get to Card 2, move back to Card 1. (Review Tip# 10, page 32)

Editing a Button

We'll edit the button and add some sound to it.
❏ To edit a button choose the *Arrow tool* from the **Tools** menu. (Fig. 6) (See Tip #14, page 34)
❏ Using the Arrow tool, double-click on the button to open it up.
❏ At the Button Appearance screen (Fig. 11) click on the button, Actions... This will take you to the Actions screen. (Fig. 13)

Playing a Sound

❏ At the Actions screen, on the Things to Do side, click on Play a Sound. This will bring you to the Tape Deck. (Fig. 15)
❏ Click on the Record Button.
❏ Speaking into the microphone say, "Welcome to France" (See Tip #15, page 34)
❏ Click the mouse to stop recording.
❏ Click on Play to listen to your recording.
❏ Click on OK.(Fig. 15)
❏ Click on Done at the Actions screen. (Fig.13)
❏ Click on Change to Browse Now when you see this message. (Fig. 16)
❏ Click on your button to go to Card 2.
❏ Now would be a good time to save. (Review Tip# 8, page 28)

Tip #17:

Changing the Color of a Card

▶ You can erase the entire background to any color you wish by choosing Erase Background from the Edit menu.

Tip #18:

The Map Button Tool

▶ This tool is great for making irregularly shaped states, provinces and countries into buttons. It works in any place that you might be able to use the fill tool. Another example where you might use this button is in making the different colored areas of a beach ball into buttons.

Tip #19:

Clicking on Position or OK

at the Button Appearance Screen

▶ Clicking on Position will bring you back to the Button Appearance screen after you've placed your button. Clicking on OK will take you directly to the Actions screen. Either method will do the job, but clicking on Position will give you the opportunity to use Position again, just in case you accidentally "drop" it, or decide to change its appearance.

Adding Another Card

❏ From the **Edit** menu, choose New card. (See Tip #17, page 36, about changing the color of a card...)

❏ Move back to card 2. (Review Tip#10)

Linking Two Cards with an Invisible Button

We'll be adding a button in the shape of France to link the two cards.

❏ Choose Add a Button from the **Objects** menu. (Fig.1) (Review Tip #11, Page 32)

❏ At the Button Appearance screen (Fig. 11) choose the map button tool. This is the bottom button on the left. (See Tip# 18, page 36)

❏ Click on Position. (See Tip # 19, page 36)

❏ You'll get a prompt telling you to click inside your shape. Click on OK.

❏ Click within France.

❏ Click on OK now that the button shape has been defined.

❏ Click on OK at the Button Appearance screen.

❏ At the Actions screen choose Next card.

❏ Choose the transition Iris open.

❏ Click on OK

❏ Click on Done.

❏ Click on your button to try it.

Copying an Image from One Card to Another

We'll be copying a portion of the map from one card and pasting it on another card.

❑ Move back to card two.

❑ Using the Selector tool, begin above and to the left of France, and drag diagonally down and to the right until you have selected an area larger than France.

❑ While you see the flashing dots, choose Copy from the **Edit** menu.

❑ Manually move to the next card, by pressing ⌘ -> or choosing *Next card* from the **Move** menu.

❑ Once you are on Card three, choose Paste from the **Edit** menu.

❑ Drag the map to the upper left-hand area of the card, leaving approximately one inch above and to the left of the map. Do not click away from the flashing dots to place the image, as we will be resizing it. If you clicked away from the image by mistake, you can select the area again with the Selector tool or choose Undo.

Resizing an Image

We'll be enlarging the map to 125%.

❑ From the **Edit** menu (Fig. 9) choose the *Effects* item to select Scale & Rotate... The area must be surrounded by flashing dots (selected).

❑ Type in 125% for the Scale factor. (Fig. 17)

❑ Click on OK.

❑ Click away from the flashing dots to turn them off.

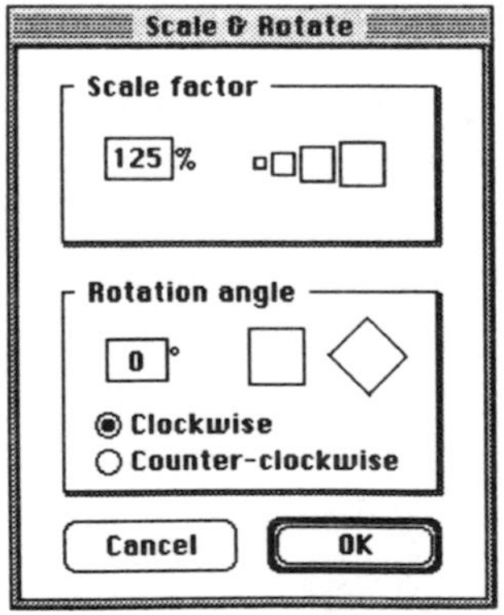

Figure 17: Scale & Rotate dialog

Tip # 20:

Graphic Objects

▶ The difference between clip art and graphic objects is that graphic objects float over the card. You cannot erase graphic objects with the eraser tool. Graphic objects must be deleted with the Arrow tool. This tool will move them, resize them, delete them and allow you to edit their actions.

▶ The reasons you would add an image as a graphic object are:

❶ They can be hidden and shown with the click of a button (HideShow NBA)

❷ They can be made to be draggable with the Browse tool (as in moveable puzzle pieces)

❸ They can be used in stacks that use Group Cards, where you want to have a common background, but unique images on each card.

❹ Since graphic objects can be moved easily with the Arrow tool, they become the better choice when working on a complex background. An example of this would be turning a painted text title into a graphic object so that it can be easily moved over a card that might have a photograph as a background. Even a simple horizontal line can be a useful graphic element when turned into a graphic object.

Tip # 21:

The Graphic Appearance Menu

▶ It is not necessary to name graphic objects unless you have more than one on a card that will be adressed by a New Button Action or a Logo script. We will name this graphic object because in the Going Further section, we will be adding a second Graphic Object to the card.

▶ You can select a frame for a graphic object if you wish. This is a neat way to create "outlined" text and other objects.

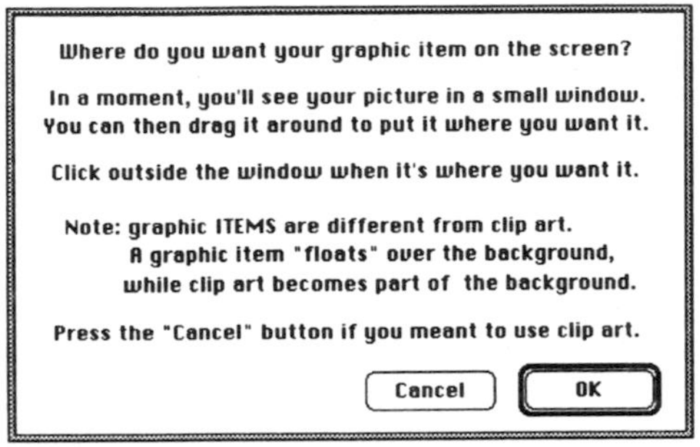

Where do you want your graphic item on the screen?

In a moment, you'll see your picture in a small window. You can then drag it around to put it where you want it.

Click outside the window when it's where you want it.

Note: graphic ITEMS are different from clip art. A graphic item "floats" over the background, while clip art becomes part of the background.

Press the "Cancel" button if you meant to use clip art.

Cancel   OK

▲▲▲
Figure 18: Graphic Object message

Adding a Graphic Object

See Tip #20, page 40
❑ From the **Objects** menu, chose Add a Graphic Object... (Fig. 1)
❑ Click on Disk file and OK if appropriate.
❑ From the HS Art folder choose Street Artist from the Photos folder.
❑ Click on Open.
❑ Using the selector tool, select the picture.
❑ Click on OK.
❑ The first time you add a Graphic Object you'll get a message telling how to place the object and reminding you that you have chosen to add a Graphic Object and not Clip Art. Click on OK. (Fig. 18)
❑ Drag the picture to the right-hand area of the card, beside the map. Click away from the flashing dots to place it there.
❑ At the Graphic Appearance menu, name the Object Artist. Choose a medium blue frame and click on the "up" arrow to get a frame width of 2. Click on OK.(See Tip#21, page 40)

Adding a Text Object

We'll be adding a container for text in which you can write and edit text easily, or import existing text.
❑ To add a text object, choose Add a Text Object from the **Objects** menu (Fig. 1).
❑ A help message will appear. Read it and click on OK.
❑ The flashing dots on your card represent the size and location of the text object you are about to create.

Tip #22:

Text Objects

▶ While you see the flashing dots, the text item can be stretched or reduced in size by dragging the mouse just inside one of the corners of the text object. The cursor will change to a two-headed diagonal arrow.

▶ If you are in the Browse mode, you'll have to switch to the Editing tool (arrow) to stretch or shrink the text item.

▶ You can change the color of one or as many words as you'd like within a text object. To change the color of the text, highlight the words you want changed by dragging the mouse across the words. Once the text has been selected, click on the new color you want in the Colors menu.

Tip #23:

Changing the Color or Style of Text in a Text Object

▶ You can change the style of one or as many words as you'd like within a text object. To change the style of the text, highlight the words you want changed by dragging the mouse across the words. Once the text has been selected, go to *Text Style* in the **Options** menu and choose either underline, italics, bold, etc.)

▶ To change the color of all of the contents in the text object, use the Arrow tool to select the text object. Once you see the flashing dots, click on the color of the text you'd prefer within the Colors menu. (You can also go to *Text Style* in the **Options** menu and change the color and/or the font there.)

❏ Drag the text object to just below the images you have added to this card. (See Tip #22, page 42)

❏ Stretch the text object so it is almost the width of the card (leaving an inch or so on the right-hand side where we will be adding a button later on) and fits between the images and the bottom of the card. (See page 23 illustration.)

❏ Click outside the text object to place it.

❏ This will bring you to the Text Appearance screen. (Fig. 19)

❏ Click on the Style button to change the size and type of the font.

❏ This will take you to the Text Style screen (Fig. 20) where you can choose a smaller font for the text . Let's choose Helvetica 14, Plain, Text Color - white, Background Color - medium blue. Click on OK.

❏ At the Text Appearance screen click on OK.

❏ Type text directly into the text object. Write a paragraph about the things you might want to see on a trip to France. **Be sure to include the phrase "street artist"**, as we will be making a button out of those words. To change the color or font of selected words or the whole text item. (See Tip #23, page 42)

❏ To let your users know that this is a hypertext link, it is a good idea to underline the words. (Review Tip #23, page 42)

Figure 19: Text Appearance dialog
▼▼▼

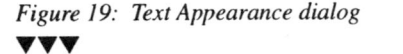

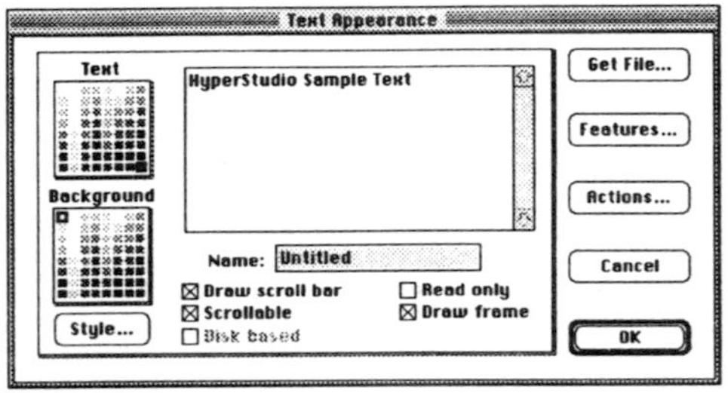

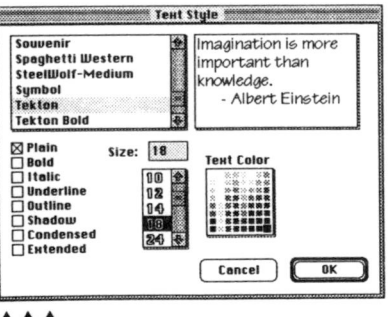

▲▲▲
Figure 20: Text Style dialog

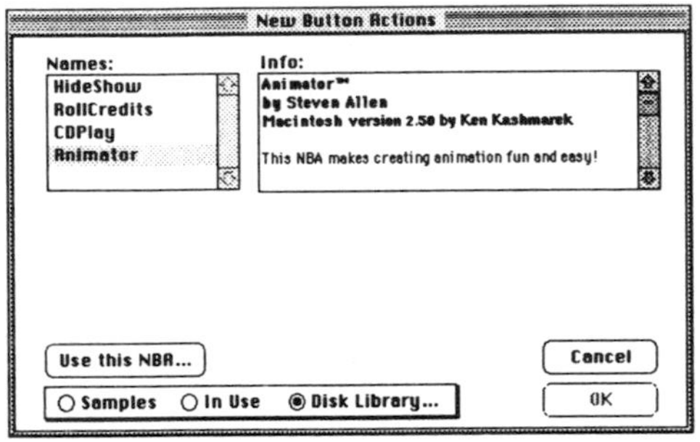

Figure 21: Selecting a New Button Action

Adding a Hypertext Link

We will now make a button out of the phrase "street artist" which will make the graphic of the artist appear.

❏ To select the phrase drag the mouse across the words "street artist".

❏ From the **Objects** menu (Fig. 1) choose Hypertext Links.

❏ Street artist will appear in the lower window. Click on Add link.

❏ Click on Action...

❏ At the Actions screen (Fig. 13), on the Things to Do side, click on New Button Actions.

❏ HideShow is a sample NBA (New Button Action) It should already be highlighted..

❏ Click on Use this NBA

❏ Name the object Artist.

❏ Click on graphic.

❏ Click on show it.

❏ Click on OK.

❏ Click on OK at the New Button Actions Screen. (Fig. 21)

❏ Click on Done at the Actions screen. (Fig. 13)

❏ Click on Done at the Hypertext Links screen.

❏ Save your stack.

Note: The first time you click on this button nothing will happen because the graphic object is already showing. What we will do is create a card action associated with this card that will hide the graphic object when leaving that card.

Tip # 24:

Ready-Made Cards

♦ The same way that you can have clip art and clip sounds, you can have clip cards. Ready-made cards can be templates for individual cards that you would like to use over and over again.

♦ To make your own ready-made card which will be added to the list, save the card as a one card stack in the Ready-Made Card folder. The next time you launch HyperStudio this card will appear in the ready-made card list.

Giving a Card an Action to Hide an Object when leaving that Card.

❑ From the **Objects** menu choose About this Card.
❑ At the About Card screen click on Things to do when: leaving this card...
❑ At the Actions menu, choose New Button Actions.
❑ The HideShow NBA will already be highlighted.
❑ Click on Use this NBA
❑ Name the object Artist.
❑ Click on graphic.
❑ Click on hide it.
❑ Click on OK.
❑ Click on OK at the New Button Actions Screen.
❑ Click on Done at the Actions screen.
❑ Click on OK at the About Card screen.
❑ Save your stack.

Adding a Ready-Made Card Template

We'll be adding a clip card, or pre-made card of a bibliography template.

❑ From the **Edit** menu. choose the item Ready-Made Cards and select the Bibliography Template. (See Tip# 24. page 46)

❑ Bibliographies are the way we can share (with other users) the source of information where we got our graphics, text, sounds and movies. In this particular project all the files were taken from the HyperSudio package. In your future projects these sources might include CD-ROM titles, URLs from the Internet, books scanned or quoted, or your name and information in cases where you created the information yourself. Bibliographies help other users get further information.

Adding a Button to Link Two Cards which Plays a Sound from a Disk File.

We'll be making a button to link two cards. Move back to card three. Notice that the graphic of the artist is now hidden! Try your Hypertext link by clicking on street artist.

❑ From the **Objects** menu choose Add a Button.

❑ At the Button Appearance screen (Fig. 11) choose the invisible button which looks like a dotted rectangle.

❑ Click on Icons.

❑ Choose the icon of the mouse. Click on OK.

❑ Click on OK at the Button Appearance screen.

❑ Drag the button to the right-hand area of the card, just beside the text object.

❑ Click away from the flashing dots to place it there.

❑ At the Actions screen choose Next card.

❑ Choose the transition Left to Right, at a Slow speed.

❑ Click on OK

❑ Choose Play a Sound at the Actions menu.

❑ Click on Disk Library... at the Tape deck. (Fig. 15)

❑ From the HS Sounds file choose ElecHarp.

❑ Click on Open.

❑ Click on OK at the Tape deck.

❑ Click on Done at the Actions screen.

❑ Click on the button to move to the Bibliography card.

Playing a QuickTime Movie

❑ Let's play a QuickTime Movie on Card 3. Manually move to Card 3.

❑ From the Objects menu (Fig. 1) choose Add a Button.

❑ Choose the invisible rectangular button.

❑ Click on Icons...

❑ Select the icon of the film strip. You'll need to scroll down to see it.

❑ Click on OK.

❑ Click on OK at the Button Appearance screen. (Fig. 11)

❑ Drag your button to the right and just below the map, and click outside the flashing dots to place it there. If you don't have enough room remember that you can move the cursor to the corner of the button until it becomes a two-headed diagonal arrow. The button can then be resized by dragging the corner. If you have already clicked outside the flashing dots, you can always resize the button later with the Arrow tool.

❑ At the Actions menu, click on Play a Movie or Video...

❑ Choose Disk file (QuickTime movies) at the Video/Movie Source screen. (Fig. 22)

❑ Click on OK.

❑ From the QuickTime Movies folder choose the Seine movie.

❑ Click on Open.

❑ The help message which appears will only appear the first time you add a QuickTime movie. Click on OK.

❑ The movie will be floating over the card, just as clip art, waiting to be placed. Drag the movie toward the left side of the card and place it over the map of France.

❑ Click outside the flashing dots to place the movie.

Figure 22: Video / Movie Source dialog
▼▼▼

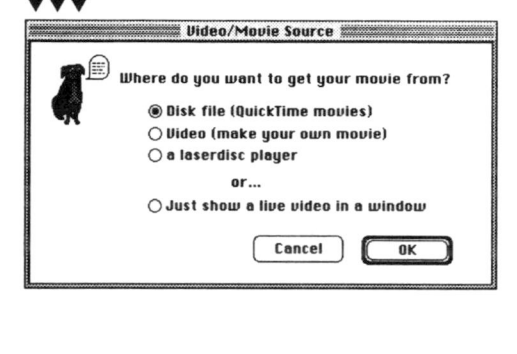

Tip #25:

QuickTime Tips

▶ A QuickTime movie can be added as a button action (when you click on the button the movie is played), or as a card action, meaning that the movie plays upon arrival to that card.

▶ Choose "Erase when done"...when you want the last frame of the movie to disappear after the movie has played.

▶ Choose "Play over objects"...when you want the movie to play over a text object, graphic object or button.

▶ Choose "Loop movie"...when you want the movie to play continuously until you leave the card.

▶ Choose "Show first frame"...if you want the first frame of the movie showing on the card. You can double-click on this image to start the movie when there is a controller bar.

▶ Choose "Use movie controller"...when you want the user to have access to the slider to control the movie or if you want to be able to start the movie by double-clicking on the first frame. You can pause the movie by clicking once on a frame.

▶ If you want a movie to dissolve & disappear after it has played, you can make a button and choose Another Card (but the connection is actually to the same card you are on), on the Places to Go side of the Actions screen, with the Transition dissolve. This button will play the movie, then dissolve into the same card, making it seem as though the movie is melting away.

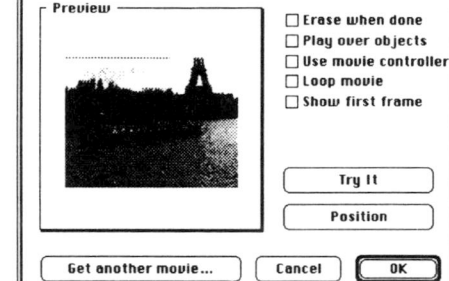

QuickTime Movies

Preview

☐ Erase when done
☐ Play over objects
☐ Use movie controller
☐ Loop movie
☐ Show first frame

Try It

Position

Get another movie...   Cancel   OK

▲▲▲
Figure 23: QuickTime Movies dialog

❑ You can preview the movie at the QuickTime Movies screen. (Fig. 23) (See Tip #25, Page 52)
❑ Click on OK.
❑ At the Actions (Fig. 13) screen click on Done.
❑ Click on your film strip button to see the movie.
❑ Save your work.

Animating the Word France

We'll write the name France on the card and make it a button to have it fly across the map.
❑ Move back to Card 2.
❑ From the **Options** menu (Fig.7) choose Text Style.
❑ Choose Chicago, size 18, red. (Fig. 20)
❑ Click on OK.
❑ Choose the T tool from the **Tools** menu.
❑ Type the name France somewhere on the top left-hand side of your card, on the blue area.
❑ From the **Objects** menu (Fig. 1) choose Add a Button.
❑ Choose the invisible button which is a dotted rectangle.
❑ Click on OK.
❑ Place the button over the word France.
❑ Click away from the flashing dots.
❑ At the Actions screen (Fig. 13) on the Things to Do side, click on New Button Actions.
❑ At the New Button Actions screen (Fig. 21) choose Animator.

Tip #26:

The Animator

▶ Releasing the mouse button will stop the path of animation while you are creating the animation. However, if you are an experienced HyperStudio user (checked in Preferences), then you will have to press the space bar to stop the animation.

Tip #27:

The Animator Screen

▶ You can speed up the animation by raising the value of the Playback rate.

▶ The choice for transparent color is used when for example a hot air balloon might be flying across the card. If you wanted the area in between the ropes to be transparent, you would select the appropriate color.

▶ You might want to hide the background on the first frame when you don't want the image which you are animating to remain stamped on that spot (such as the state name you have typed).

▶ An instance where you'd hide the graphic on the last frame might be if you were showing a car driving into a garage.

▶ If you need your animation to end in a specific spot, begin your animation on that spot and create the animation backwards. Once it is done, choose Reverse direction in the Edit Path button.

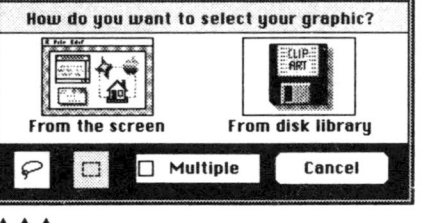

Figure 24: Animator's graphic source dialog

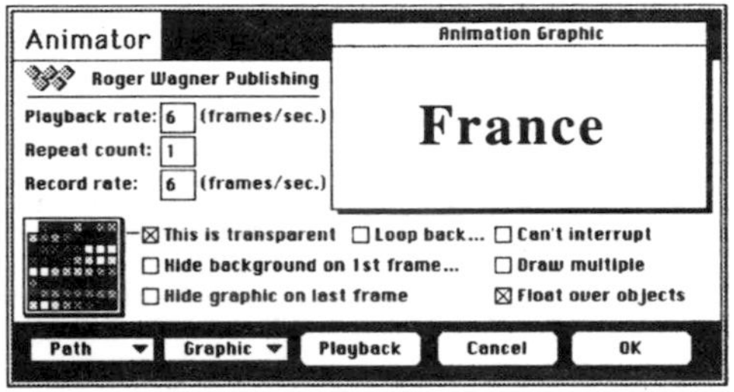

Figure 25: Animator's preview screen

❑ Click on Use this NBA.
❑ Click on From the screen (Fig. 24), because the image we want to animate is on our card, rather than from a disk file.
❑ The cursor becomes a crosshair. Use it to select the name France. Begin above and to the left of the word and drag diagonally down and to the right.
❑ This image (the word France) becomes the cursor. Dragging the mouse with the mouse button down will create the animation path. Releasing the mouse button will stop the animation. (See Tip #25, page 54)
❑ Drag the mouse to move the name until it is over France, and then release the mouse button.
❑ This Animator screen (Fig. 25) is where you can preview your animation by clicking on Playback, speed it up, slow it down, select a new graphic, recreate or edit the path of animation. (See Tip # 26, page 54)
❑ Click on OK.
❑ Click on OK at the New Button Actions screen. (Fig. 21)
❑ Click on Done at the Actions screen. (Fig. 13)
❑ Try your button.
❑ Save your stack.

Congratulations! You have completed your first project! Move back to Card one and click through your stack. You might want to create buttons which move back to previous cards, or add some artwork with the paint tools. You now know the core set of skills that most people use in creating HyperStudio projects.

Tip #28:

Using Gradients

▶ Imagine having a border on a card, such as the border in *Dingbats 2*. (Imagine that the artwork had been deleted using the Selector tool and then pressing the delete key.) You can fill that center area with a gradient:

❶ Choose the Lasso and do an option-click. To do this press the option key while you click the mouse within that white area. This will turn the lasso into an expanding lasso, thereby selecting the inner white area.

❷ When you see the flashing dots, choose **Gradients**... within the **Effects** item in the **Edit** menu.

❸ Choose the gradient pattern and then apply it.

▶ You can also use the gradient effect to fill small, hard to fill areas, such as a mosaic type pattern.

❶ Lasso the area.

❷ Choose the same color for the Top and Bottom of the gradient and then click on Apply.

Figure 26: Turning selected art into a graphic
▼▼▼

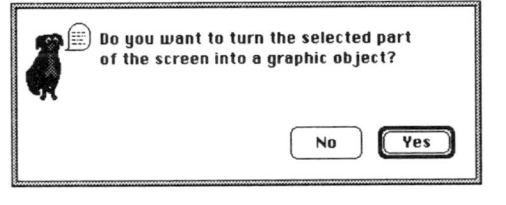

Going Further

Playing QuickTime Movies in Irregular Shapes

Here's a neat trick that doesn't take a lot of steps, but is really impressive! Move to Card three. Let's play the QuickTime movie within the shape of France.

❏ Before we begin, here is what we will do. We will turn the selected map into a stencil, with France being the transparent hole. Then we will turn the map into a graphic object, so that it covers the square edges of the movie, making it seem that the movie itself is an irregular shape.

❏ Using the fill tool, make France white. France must be white because whatever color that you start the lasso on becomes the transparent color within the selected area. The card is white, so France must be white.

❏ Using the lasso tool, encircle the map.

❏ While you see the flashing dots, choose *Add a Graphic Object* from the **Objects** menu.

❏ You will be asked whether you want to turn the selected image into a Graphic object. Click on Yes. (Fig. 26)

❏ Click on OK at the Graphic Appearance screen. You do not need to give this object a name.

❏ Choose the *Browse* tool from the **Tools** menu.

❏ Click on the button to play your movie!

Using Gradients

Move to Card 1.

❏ Using the lasso tool encircle the title "France".

❏ Press the option key and drag the mouse slightly to the left to make a

Figure 27: The Gradients dialog

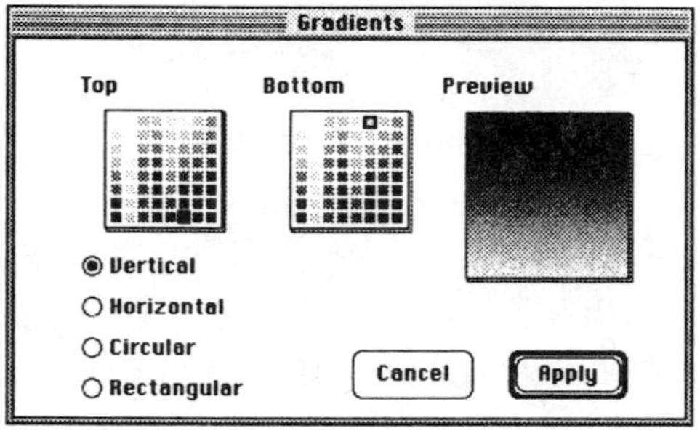

quick copy of the title.

❑ Do not click away from the flashing dots.

❑ From the **Edit** menu choose Gradients... from within the *Effects* item.

❑ Choose the darkest blue for the Top, and the lightest blue for the Bottom, at the Gradients dialog. (See fig. 27)

❑ Choose Vertical.

❑ Click on Apply.

❑ Do not click away from the flashing dots.

❑ The cursor becomes a 4-way directional arrow as you move across the letters. This means you can drag the selected area. Drag the mouse slightly up and to the left, just slightly offset from the original title, creating a shadow.

❑ Click away from the flashing dots to place the title. (See Tip #28, Page 56)

Advanced Techniques

In this chapter:

Once you are comfortable with the basic HyperStudio skills, you should spend some time exploring this chapter. There are instances where you can combine several simple elements to create very impressive effects. Simple to use should not be confused with lack of depth and sophistication!

Advanced Techniques

If you have used HyperStudio's animator NBA, and have set yourself as an experienced user, you will have noticed that the animation can take place behind or in front of objects. In this instance we want the animation to take place behind the object. The important thing to remember is that graphic objects float over the card on another layer. Pieces of clip art, painted text or any selected area can be turned into graphic objects. Keeping this in mind, you can imagine objects on the screen that the animation would pass behind, yet painted areas of the card that it would pass in front of.

Basic Procedure:

❶   Draw some simple artwork or lettering on the card.

❷ Lasso the portions of the artwork or letters where you want to have the animation pass behind.

❸ While the flashing dots still surround the selected area, choose Add a Graphic Object from the Objects menu.

❹ Turn the selected area into the graphic object.

❺ Create a button which uses the Animator NBA to move something across the screen.

❻ Click on your button to try it.

See the Advanced Techniques stack in the HyperStudio Home Stack, where this technique is called layered animation.

Use Graphics for Titles

It's a good idea to turn your painted titles into graphic objects. This way you can manipulate titles on top of a busy background or digitized photograph. You can also have them outlined.

Basic Procedure:

❶ Type some text with the T tool.

❷ Encircle the title with the lasso. This will surround each letter with the flashing dots.

❸ Choose Add a Graphic Object from the Objects menu.

❹ Turn the selected area into the graphic object.

That's it!

Create Graphics with Actions

Graphic objects can have actions associated with them! This is more efficient than the alternative of drawing an image and then creating an invisible button over it.

Basic Procedure:

❶ Draw or import some artwork.

❷ Once it has been selected with either the square selector tool, the circular selector tool, or the lasso, choose Add a Graphic Object from the Objects menu.

❸ Turn the selected image into a graphic object.

❹ At the Graphic Appearance screen click on Actions... to get to the Actions screen where you can choose the actions you'd like associated with your graphic.

Play QuickTime Movies
in Interesting Shapes

Since graphic objects float over the card on another layer, and since graphic objects can be any shape, they can be placed over square movies to hide their corners, making it seem as though the movie itself was an irregular shape.

Basic Procedure:

❶ Create a stencil-like image by using the lasso to capture an image of your map with the county cut out. The lasso does this automatically whenever the inside color is the same as the outside color .

❷ While the flashing dots still surround the stencil, choose Add a Graphic Object from the Objects menu.

❸ Turn the selected image into a graphic object.

❹ Create a button which will play a QuickTime movie. Be sure that Play over objects remains "unchecked" in the QT Preview window.

This procedure appears in the step-by-step tutorial project about France. You can also see this in the Tutorial Project stack in the Sample Projects folder.

Tricks With Transitions:
Revealing Text

You already know that transitions are the special effects which you see when going from one card to another. By using a left to right transition, a new line of text can be revealed at each click of the button!

Things Appearing Magically

By creating two cards with the same background and then adding some new things to the second card, you can make those things seem to appear magically with the Transition, Dissolve.

Easy Animations with Transitions

If you'd like to create a rising curtain or window shade effect, use the Bottom to Top or Top to Bottom transitions. If the two cards are nearly identical but represent the up and down position, the transition will give the illusion of a computer animation.

See the HyperStudio Journal which is shown in the commercial section of HyperStudio.

More Ideas!

Cookie Cutters & Copiers

For this trick imagine a boldly written word or a solid shape. Now imagine picking up a pattern from a picture so that the letters are written in that pattern, or the shape is filled with that pattern. To do this we have to create a card with a pattern on it. Then we have to have a working card to write our text or make our shape. What we'll do is lasso the text, copy it, and bring it over to the pattern. We'll then pick up the pattern from the first card and bring our new text back.

Basic Procedure:

❶ Type your title using a bold, chunky font.

❷ Add a new card and import an appropriate background (a gradient, photograph, or tiling of small clip art).

❸ Move to the title card.

❹ Lasso the Title

❺ Copy it.

❻ Move to the card with the nice background.

❼ Paste the title, but do not click away from the flashing dots.

❽ Press **Option-Command-C** the cookie copier command. You will know that you have been successful if the letters become transparent within the flashing dots.

❾ Move back to your title card and paste the new title. Don't worry about the flashing dots on the other card.

❿ Drag the new title just slightly above and to the left of the original title, creating a drop shadow.

You can see this in the Advanced Techniques section of the Home Stack.

QuickTime Movies - Disappearing

Did you know that you can have a QuickTime movie disappear after it plays? Not only can it disappear, but it can disappear using the transition of your choice.

Basic Procedure:

At the Button Actions menu, choose *Play a Movie or video...*and also choose Another card on the Places To Go side of the menu.

❷ When you select the other card to connect to, make the connection to the card you are on. (You simply click on OK when you see the card with the movie on it.)

❸ Choose a transition. Dissolve works nicely.

❹ This will cause the movie to play, and then HyperStudio will go to the same card it is on, thereby refreshing the screen, after the selected transition. Try it!

Wondering How to Erase the Text
in GhostWriter?

Ghost Writer is a neat NBA that will automatically "type" words into a text object. GhostWriter has an option to "backspace", which can be used to erase the text when you're done, but it's not very efficient, or visually appealing.

A better approach is to use the TextMover NBA to move the contents of an empty text object into the place where GhostWriter just "wrote", thus erasing it all! This is usually done by a button that moves to the next card, but can be done with any button that serves your purpose.

Basic Procedure:

❶ Set up the text object that you want the text to appear in, and give it a specific name, like "MyMessage".

❷ Create a button (probably using the Automatic Timer feature in the Actions dialog) that uses GhostWriter to make your text appear.

❸ Create an empty text object somewhere else on that card or in your stack (at the end of the stack is a good place) named "Empty".

❹ Make a button that goes to the next card, and add to it the TextMover NBA. In the command box for TextMover, you would just enter the lines:

Empty

MyMessage

When the button is clicked to go to the next card, it will also erase the MyMessage box by moving the empty contents of Empty into it!

An Experienced User
Might Like to Know:

▶ Stacks in 16 colors take half the memory of 256-color stacks.

▶ If you are using the same background on lots of cards, group cards are a good idea.

A Way to Refresh the Screen:

▶ Buttons made with a connection to Another Card, and choosing the same card you are on, will restore the screen. This would be good for a card which played a frame animation. If you made a "reset" button going to the same card, the words would disappear, making the screen ready for the next user. If you had scrolling text item that had been scrolled down, it would be reset back to the top as well.

Setting the Text Color
of a Button:

▶ When a button is selected, choosing a color from the Colors menu will set the text color inside the button.

The Color of the Text and Background
within a Text Object:

▶ If you select an entire text object with an editing tool, choosing a color from the Colors menu will set the color for all the text in that text object. If you hold down the Option key while you choose a color, then the background color for the entire text object will be set.

Shortening a Shape:

▶ If you have a rectangular shape (for example, a rounded solid border around a blank interior), there are some tricks for lengthening or shortening the shape as needed. To shorten (either vertically or horizontally), just use the square selector tool, and select the horizontal or vertical half of your shape. Then slide the selected image back on top of the existing graphic. The effect will be to make the shape a little shorter.

Lengthening a Shape:

▶ To make a graphic longer, hold down the Option key when you press the mouse button to start dragging the selected region. This will make a copy that when overlaid with a slight offset, will extend the graphic. Both these techniques are similar to what you would do with wallpaper when trying to fit a specific-sized area. This is a little difficult to describe with words, but is pretty easy to grasp if demonstrated. If you can't get someone to show you, experiment a little and you'll probably be able to see what we're talking about.

Create a Text Object
or Use the T Tool?

▶ Remember that a text object uses much less memory than painting words on the screen. Also, with a text object, you can go back and insert letters, and easily edit the words later on if you wish. Try creating a text field with no rectangle frame, no scrolling, no scroll bar, and read-only. Then, select the text object with the pointer or text-item tool (Tools menu), and choose Set Background Color from the Options menu. Set the background color to the same color as is behind your text field. The result you should get is that the text is now indistinguishable from a title or other text you would have "painted" there. The trade-offs are that text objects take much less memory, and can be edited later. On the other hand, the necessary font must be in the Fonts folder of your startup disk when this stack is accessed (or when your ultimate end user uses the stack), or else you'll get some other font, instead.

Transparent Text Objects:

▶ Transparent Text Objects - As an Experienced user, you will be able to choose Transparent as a feature of your text object. Transparent text objects allow you to see through them, so that the background underneath shows through.

Choose this feature when you want text showing over a non-solid background. Transparent text objects are not scrollable.

Color Replace: ▶ This is a handy effect that will manipulate all the color pixels in any selected (lasso, circular or rectangle) area. Having selected a part of the graphic background, just choose Effects in the Edit menu. One of the choices will be Replace colors . You have the option of either replacing all occurrences of one color with another, or swapping two colors. Replacing is an easy way to change (for example), a green arrow into a blue arrow, without having to use the fill tool or the magnifying glass. The exchange color option can quickly "invert" an image. For example, swap black and white (or a light/dark color pair) for an interesting effect.

Pop-up Objects: ▶ On some occasions, you may wish you could have an image "pop up" on a card when a button is pressed. There are two ways to do this. The first, "brute force" method is to just create a second card, that looks identical to the first, except that it has an additional text object, graphic object, or whatever on it. A button on the first card then moves to the second, with the "fastest" transition, to create the "pop-up" effect. Another button can move back to the first card to make the pop-up item "disappear".

Another approach is to use "Export screen" (File menu) to save an image of the screen with the word, graphic, etc. that you want to pop up. Save it with a name that ends in a number, such as "Lion.1". What you are creating is essentially a one-frame animation. Now, create the triggering button, and have it do an animation. Select your single graphic image as the "animation" to play, and crop the image as necessary so that just the image you want appears at the desired location on the screen. Use a Rate and Repeat Count of "1". The advantage of 1-frame animation pop-ups is that they are very fast. To make the image go away,

create a button that "moves to another card", but have it just move to the card that is already there. The effect will be to refresh the original screen, thus erasing the pop-up item. You can combine multiple buttons, each with a pop-up graphic for very interesting effects. Imagine a "Mr. Potato Head" where you add different parts, or pictures of a variety of animals in Africa, etc.

Ask Addy

In this chapter:

Not sure about the way to do something? Perhaps Addy can help you. Even if you are an experienced Hyperstudio user you might pick up a useful tip in this section.

I'd Like to:

Know what a stack is!

✔ A stack is series of cards which are linked together with buttons (hot spots on the screen where you can click the mouse to make things happen).

✔ On these cards you can add buttons, text, animation, graphics, show QuickTime movies and play a laserdisc video. Try the tutorial which will take you through making your first stack.

Start my own stack.

✔ To begin a new stack, choose *New Stack* from the **File** Menu. You will be given one card with a white background.

Know how many cards I should put in a stack.

✔ It's a good idea to button together lots of little stacks rather than creating one giant stack. Why not make 20 the maximum number of cards in a stack? If you were writing a book, you'd split it into chapters, so why not divide your projects into little stacks?

Look at a stack I've already saved.

✔ Choose *Open Stack* from the **File** menu. You'll be shown the window of what's in the HyperStudio folder. Your stack should be there, perhaps in a folder you've named My Stacks. It's a good idea to create a folder where you keep your own stacks.

Remove a button!

✔ To delete a button you have to select it with the ▶. Once it is selected, press the *delete* key.

Fix a piece of clip art

that was pasted

with a white square around it.

✔ If you have selected your clip art with the ⌐⌐, rather than the ℘, then you will take the rectangle drawn by the Selector tool as well. You can always use the 🖌 to fill in this white space with the color of your background. If you are adding clip art to a background with lots of artwork on it already, then use the ℘.

Know why Undo didn't work

when I tried it!

✔ Undo works right after you've made the mistake. It undoes the last thing done. If you make a mistake and then click somewhere else...too late! Learn the keyboard shortcut ⌘-Z to Undo and fix mistakes quickly.

Tear off the Tools Menu.

✔ Move the mouse over the word **Tools** (in the menu bar) until it changes to an arrow. Pull the menu down and keep dragging until the menu tears away. You will see a dotted outline. Releasing the mouse will set the menu on your card. Tearing off the menu is a must if you want to double-click on the art tool icons. You can also tear off the Colors menu.

Erase something

drawn with a paint tool

or written with the (paint) Text tool.

1. Use the ✏ set to the same color as the background, or

2. Do fine erasing using the magnifier, or

3. Select an area with the ⌐⌐ and then press the *delete* key.

*Take text from one card
and put it somewhere else.*

✔ That's called cutting and pasting. Select the text object with the Arrow Tool. Choose *Cut* from the **Edit** menu. Create a new text object on the new card. Choose *Paste* from the **Edit** menu.

✔ If you only wanted to cut and paste part of the text, that is also possible. Select the text you want, by dragging the mouse across the words. Choose *Cut*. Set the cursor down in the new text item. Choose *Paste*. Remember the ⌐⌐ is for selecting artwork or painted text, while the ▶ is for selecting buttons, text items and graphic items. Use the ⬆ to select a portion of text that you want to cut or copy.

*Find my buttons.
They are invisible
and I can't see them.*

✔ Press the *option* key and the ⌘ -key at the same time. You'll see your invisible buttons! If you don't want people to see your invisible buttons when they press option -⌘ then lock your stack.

*Know more about
the Roll Credits NBA.*

✔ You don't need to enter the name of the text item unless you have more than one text item on the card. If there is only one text item on the card, Roll Credits will automatically find it.

✔ The total scroll rate is the number of pixels per scroll times the number of steps per second. This means that 3 pixels at 10 steps per second is the same as 1 pixel at 30 steps per second.

Other Technologies....

Can I use a Sony LDP? ✔ HyperStudio has built in support for Pioneer laserdisc players. If you have a Sony please call The HyperStudio Network at 609-466-3196.

Sound Advice....
Can I play audio CDs? ✔ One of the sample NBAs is CDPlay. This NBA will put a remote control on the screen from which you can set the start and stop times for your CD. This is also the place where you can make a button to eject the CD.

I want a sound to loop,
or play over & over.
Is this possible? ✔ Yes! Create a button which plays a QuickTime movie. Instead of choosing a movie file, choose the sound file which you want to work with. You'll notice a "Convert" button in the dialog box. This will turn the sound into a QuickTime movie. At the QuickTime preview screen, there's a "Loop movie" choice. Choose it.

Have sound on a card. ✔ Make a button! At the Actions menu choose *Play a Sound*. Buttons can do things without having connections to other cards.

Know if it is possible
to play 2 sounds at the same time.
What I had in mind was
some music playing
and a recording of my voice
announcing the title of my stack. ✔ I'm glad you asked! Sure you can do it! If you set yourself as an *Experienced User* in the *Preferences* menu item, when you get to the tape recorder, you will see a choice called *Background Sound*. This means that it is a sound which will keep on playing regardless of whether you start a second sound. If you record your music as a background sound and your voice as a regular sound, this will work!